Young Projects

Figure—Cast—Frame

Young Projects
Figure—Cast—Frame

Bryan Young

Foreword by Nader Tehrani

Contributions by Dana Barnes, Paola Lenti,
Sean Canty, Jeannette Kuo, Hashim Sarkis

M

Young Projects' Immaculate Disfiguration

Nader Tehrani

The figure features prominently in the history of art, and the varied image of the human body from the Egyptian, Greek, Roman, and modern eras registers the changing modes of representation of their respective times. The real of the human figure, in all cases, remains faithful to the attributes of the body, and yet the tools, techniques, and attitudes of different times allow for that real to be reconfigured in each instance. In architecture, the "real" is embodied in oft archaic and elemental structures and archetypes whose repeated presence over centuries gives evidence of the architectural figure. And, indeed, that figure features prominently in the work of Young Projects, and yet it is paired with an appeal to distortion, anomaly, and disfiguration.

In the firm's work, the figure appears in two separate though codependent forms: first, through the disciplinary terms of typology, and second, through the allusive and organic mechanisms of sculpted forms. If the former takes shape around recognizable architectural elements, such as rooms or gabled

The pulled plaster surface and the folded stainless-steel screen in the Pulled Plaster House project display a flirtation with referentiality, drawing in the "curtain" through its many guises, while channeling the actual expression of the respective surfaces through the very means and methods of their fabrication—often developed as part of the research. Bryan Young's conversation with Dana Barnes speaks in more detail about this aspect of the work, but suffice it to say that the focus on the architectural figure finds itself at many scales.

roof structures, the second adopts abstract geometries that escape immediate semantic associations. Equally important, the typological figure is called on to impose organizational principles of composition (whether in repetition, aggregation, or apparent disarray), while the organic figure is adopted to form a blanket that ties all the fragments together, in effect to demonstrate the unity of the work as a single body. While this dichotomy is evident at the scale of the buildings, there is also another realm in which Young Projects translates this preoccupation, that is the detail and the material agency that serves as its catalytic agent.

At the core of its intellectual interests, the firm wishes to demonstrate that the serendipities of site, program, or client whimsy are not necessarily the substance of detrimental compromise, but instead the conduit through which disciplinary virtuosity may be exercised. The immaculate perfection of its craft belies the complexity and contradictions that underly its work. It also reveals a discussion on tectonics that underscores the intricacies surrounding the technical and visual performance of the work of architecture. In effect, the apparent simplicity of these formal and spatial ideas conceals the very evidence of the problems being solved behind the scenes. In this sense, among others, there are two extreme paradigms around which architecture commonly revolves: the first, an architecture of appearance where ideas are revealed in their pure expression; and the second, an inquiry into the systems that motivate architecture, that which you discover "under the hood." There are many architects who shine in one of these areas, but very few attend to both. Young Projects excels at bringing these two paradigms into conversation. With this introduction, I hope to bring some of these issues to the surface, not only to reveal the sophisticated intellectual terrain through which the work navigates, but also to demonstrate how the work produces new forms of knowledge through architecture itself: its forms, spaces, and materialities.

The typological figure, then, has multiple functions. Its generic off-the-shelf qualities appeal to the practical, the buildable, and the construction trades that will be on the receiving end of drawing sets. But also, its conventionality assures a legibility to broader audiences, and herein lies a possible semantic bias in its thinking. The work speaks to a language of types that span across history, borrowing from forms both canonical and regional. More importantly, the malleability of the typological figure, in its ability to absorb distortion, enables the introduction of spatial transformations that are at the core of Young Projects' operations.

There is a consistency in the firm's body of work, and its methodological tropes work across scales and programs, demonstrating the range of processes its design inquiries embrace. And while you witness this range from an inspection of its objects, surfaces, installations, and buildings, you can use the key projects featured in this book as detailed case studies. The triad encompassing the Guest House (2019), the Six Square House (2020), and the Retreat House (2019) serves as a productive set of projects through which its ideas may be embodied. An outlier to these projects is the Glitch House (2018), which also deserves mention here, as it helps to establish a critical relationship between its constructive parts and the whole.

Of these, the Guest House is the most elemental in scale, in expression, and in the operations it entails. Composed of four identical cubes, sandwiched by floor and roof planes, it is conceptually straightforward. Designed around a radius, the nested cubes are rotated such that their primary window planes alternatively focus on two trees, whose locations vary from the radius of the roof and floor plane. This discrepancy serves as an alibi to both contain and expose these cubes within the floor and roof planes, effectively subsuming the cubes to the authority of the large radius on one side, while objectifying the cubic figures on the other side, nested within smaller radial geometries whose function is to graft them together seamlessly. The zones between these cubes serve as a third space, neither of

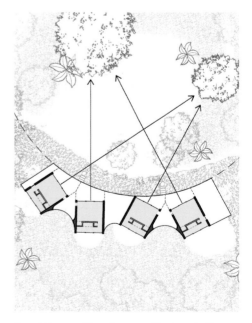

Guest House, siting diagram with views to ficus trees, Dominican Republic

the larger radial geometry nor of the generic cube. These trapezoidal voids serve as a threshold into the structure, amplifying the perspectival focus they project outside of the building into the landscape, while adopting the thickened mass of those walls to shape a tertiary space. Concurrently, if the flat terrain were to seem relatively benign as a foundation, the floor and roof planes gain subtle inflections to situate their spatial performance. Accordingly, the floor is fashioned as a monolithic plane rooted firmly in the ground, an approximate offset of the roof. If the ground is normative in its accommodation of stairs, benches, and terraces, the roof plane contains a geometric twist—a vaulting so shallow that it is perceived as an entasis at best. If the roof is seen as flat, then the ceiling is read as if carved from the mass of the entire ensemble. Abstract in its finish, the plaster denies the building of materiality, and, as such, the structure oscillates between two readings—one subtractive and the other additive.

In inspecting the Six Square House and the Retreat House, there emerges a dialectic that is worthy of rehearsing for this analysis. Both houses partake in the paired commitment to the figurative and configurative conundrum that Young Projects wills on them, but they are played out in starkly different ways. While both plans are composed of a series of cellular aggregations of rooms, in the Six Square House, the figure of those very rooms manifests as an extrusion, thus revealing the dissonance of self-similar figures in the landscape. In contrast, the plan of the Retreat House conceals its cellular orchestration by the introduction of service spaces—or poché zones—that buffer one room in relation to the next. But even more critically, the aggregated rooms are subsumed by the larger figure of a roof that absorbs the intricacy of the planning into a larger and singular form: the courtyard

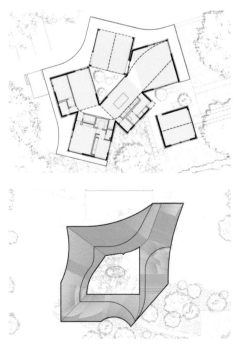

Six Square House, plan diagram, Bridgehampton, New York

Retreat House, roof plan, Dominican Republic

type. Contorted within and without, it absorbs the many natural forces—trees, topography, setbacks—that form the site.

These two houses recall many historical examples that have rehearsed common questions, forming the very ground on which Young Projects is now walking and which it seeks to overturn. Consider Louis Kahn's Fisher House (1967) and the tense relationship between its two extruded volumes. It was the very precursor for Kahn's proposal for the Dominican Motherhouse (1968), whose confetti of intersecting buildings appear randomly dispersed within a larger court, though they are in fact absolute in their precise configuration. Kahn's compositional informality belies a razor-sharp configurative stubbornness, the very mechanism that forces the thresholds between building masses to conjoin with tight reciprocity. And while these compositions are held together by the frame of a larger court, each building mass maintains its autonomy, never obligated to cohere to a broader whole.

This very sensibility is translated further into a myriad of practices today, from SANAA to Sou Fujimoto and from Junya Ishigami to MOS Architects. And yet, none has taken on the architectural imperative of uniting disaggregated volumes into a larger figure, because, in great part, of the sheer difficulty of achieving both technical and conceptual reconciliation. Most practices have escaped the syntactic meticulousness with which Kahn attended to the plan, but all denied the compositional unity that may conjoin a difficult synthesis.

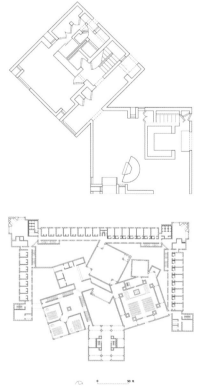

The Six Square House is unique in this lineage. Its plan is, in fact, four plus two volumes. The garage forms a separate volume, almost generic in its massing, set to the side, while forming a critical edge for the entry court. In turn, four other volumes are joined in an open

Fisher House, ground floor plan, Louis I. Kahn, Hatboro, Pennsylvania, USA, 1967

The Dominican Motherhouse, plan, Louis I. Kahn, Media, Pennsylvania, USA, 1965-68

plan wrapped around a triangular court, leaving the last volume to serve as an outdoor porch extending the court into the garden beyond. The spatial invention that is the result of this conjointment is described by the delicate balance of this space in its sinuous singularity and the simultaneous recognition of its aggregate parts.

Clever in their planning, these volumes simulate the pragmatism of New England farmhouse structures, whereby volumes are unselfconsciously added on over time as need arises. And yet, there is possibly nothing more self-conscious than the composition of the five volumes that form the main spaces of Six Square House, not only in the way they remain apart, but also more importantly in the way they are brought together. To this end, the roof serves as the house's main protagonist; mimicking the simplicity of the garage, a pure gabled structure set on the same concrete base as the house, the five volumes are conceived as simple gable roofs, yet the ridgeline that would normally be centered on each volume is reoriented in order to conjoin with its neighboring volumes. This seemingly simple decision produces what amounts to the radical complexity of this geometric challenge, and in turn the visual drama it unleashes. The shifting ridgeline also forces the roof to meet the edge walls in key moments of junction, forcing curvatures of the roofline, the result of ruled surfaces, whose cornice lines come to a perfectly delineated set of corners. If the classical work of architecture is premised on notions of resolution and unity, and in contrast informal works are premised on the aggregate effects of serendipity, Six Square House uses the techniques of the latter but with the agendas of the former. The ambiguity that is its result is itself a wonder, not only a riddle to unlock, but also a visual delight to unveil.

The Retreat House, in its mediation with natural elements, forms a courtyard that is ambiguously bipolar in its composition. In what seems a perfect tension, the plan appears to be a sinuous deformation of what might have been a rectangular court or, otherwise interpreted, a plan whose picturesque promenade is a mere index of the natural conditions onto which it has been transposed. Lest this be confused with the notion that the plan emanated naturally from its surroundings, far from it. The artifice from which such scenographic meanders unfold cannot be left to nature, but rather to precisely the poised compositional hand that balances motivated ambivalence. The figure of the courtyard is the result of a strategic framing of a Ficus tree, and yet it departs from the traditional trope that attempts to theatricalize nature. Sverre Fehn's surreal framing of a bosque of trees on the Biennale Grounds (1962) and Albert Frey's encapsulation of the boulder in House II (1964) are just two such extraordinary examples. Others, like those of Young Projects, depart from this overt sensationalism. Herzog & de Meuron's early Plywood House (1985) gains its logic from the tree it confronts, folding inward, as it were. The figure of the house is unmistakably linked to the tree, and yet it maintains a more cerebral rapport as it translates the wood into the complex arrangement of tectonic engagements: the timber of the floor beams, the plywood siding, the wooden louvers, as well as the wood-clad interiors. In effect, the narrative of the tree is adopted to focus back on the house itself. Similarly, in the Retreat House, the focus is on the ineffable relationship between the figural court, the precision of its geometry, and its uncanny confrontation with the facts of construction. Indeed, it is this relationship that translates Young Projects' focus on part to whole equations into tectonic terms. Beyond the scale of the room and the roof, it is the material unit that is required to negotiate the curvilinear terms of the sinuous plans and sections that describe these houses.

The Six Square and Retreat House share a common tectonic strategy in their insistent mono-materiality: the wooden slats and struts, respectively, wrap from the surface of the facade onto the roof. In what would be deemed as a defiant and improbable act in another era, this treatment is an integral part of rainscreen tectonics. If classical tectonics would mandate articulated formal and material transitions from base to wall and roof conditions, it was premised on the actual technical performance of those junctions, effectively protecting the structure from inclement weather. The details of that architecture were an embodiment of

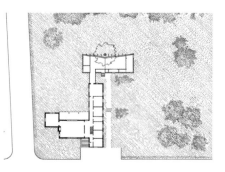

Plywood House, plan, Herzog & de Meuron, Bottmingen, Switzerland, 1984–1985

tectonics in an era of material and functional differentiation. Here, under the regime of the rainscreen, the waterproofing membrane around the building expresses the necessity of that suppression and offers the possibility of a breathing envelope that accepts water through its pores while protecting the membrane underneath from the sun's rays. From a technical perspective, this has required a substantial set of architectural alignments in the zone of the substrate to ensure the disciplined flashing of drainage pipes, window details, and corners. And what is possibly most fascinating is that what seems to take the challenge out of the very difficulty of architecture is here recast into geometric terms. The alignment of cladding elements around curvilinear corners requires the constant recalibration of alignments, which are reconciled by the tolerances between slats, ensuring the visual continuity of lines.

The exception to these projects, while also preoccupied with the architectural figure, is the Glitch House. Composed of an organic relationship between the concrete blocks from which the house is fabricated and the shape of the building, the eccentricity of the house emerges from a latent organizational trope that is part of the DNA of the concrete blocks. That is, while normative walls may be laid out as running bonds, stacked bonds allow for a planimetric corbelling that objectifies the block when viewed at a diagonal rake. Thus, this house plays into this mannerism at two scales, whereby the slipped diagonal blocks produce the syncopated massing of the structure. If this were not enough in itself, the deliberate graphic superposition of colored cement tiles on the blocks allows the building to virtually disappear into the foliage of the landscape. A stealth camouflage, the integrally colored cement tile is composed of dappled variations, the impressions of which alert us to its pointillist tendencies, if only to conceal the geometry of its massing. The detail is somehow at the core—not so much the afterthought, nor the finishing touch—of Young Projects' intellectual game. Indeed, with this house the firm reveals that the *detail* may serve as the inaugural moment for all of these structures, forming the rules through which geometries and forms may be played out.

The exploitation of the figure is, of course, not unique to Young Projects. Architects from Álvaro Siza to Herzog & de Meuron have displayed the mastery of formal dexterity though which building types and their requisite rituals get cultivated top-down. Siza's Santa Maria Church (1996) is a paradigmatic example; the figure of the basilica is partially referenced in the body of the church. Others whose sensibilities sway toward the molecular scale of the detail demonstrate the intelligence of material systems that may form architecture's rules, bottom-up—another early Herzog & de Meuron project, the Ricola Storage Building (1987), serves as an important catalyst in this arena. And yet, few architects have been able to work simultaneously top-down and bottom-up, crafting an intellectual bridge between the two while evading the very clichés that limit each method. Young Projects' ability to operate between these very scales is its most important weapon. In fact, the work of the firm plays a devious trick on us. Less prone to the assaults of the avant-garde, it instead prefers to seduce us and lure us into its trap. Much like the Trojan horse, its arsenal is concealed within a figure that is not only intelligible but also alluring. The firm encodes its figures with the very genetic makeup that assures their delivery. And deliver it does.

Upon review, Young Projects' young projects—those from our first decade—seem quite disparate from each other as completed buildings. Some projects express explicit interest in form, geometry, and structure, yet others could easily be described as restrained and minimal. There is a unique, deep interest in material experimentation and the production of alluring sensations, but the spectrum for this inquiry extends from celebrating animated patterns of color and texture to embracing homogenous or immaterial abstraction. The myriad qualities that describe the work are often put in tension with each other, working at times in opposition, to strangely nullify an effect, and at times in harmony, exaggerating an impression.

We've come to understand that the unifying thread across our projects may be exactly this desire to create multiple oscillations within and between hierarchical readings and definable characteristics, be they spatial, material, or typological. As presented in this book, spatial oscillations often require establishing an organizational protocol from which subsequent reading may stray or conflict. Material oscillations might be better understood as material ambiguities in which intrinsic qualities are revealed without clarifying the source. Typological oscillations adopt a building convention, either vernacular or structural, but shift to propose divergent organizations and geometries.

A brief survey might best begin with the Glitch House. The house establishes a proto-architecture that is intimately conscious of context, aware of its site, budget, builder, inhabitant, life cycle, and climate. The pixelated skin of the Glitch House eerily vibrates in the jungle. The sensation of optical glitches is the result of studiously calibrated patterns, shapes, and colors on the tiles interfering with temporal solar conditions that create shifting shadows and illumination. As shadows meander in and out of focus, the surface pattern and geometry of the facade also subtly transforms within the tropical landscape.

The playful surrealism of the Glitch House bounces between seemingly contradictory extremes, ultimately creating a bizarre structure that is at once vernacular and foreign, natural and artificial. To come upon this uncanny building, one is compelled to move around the structure, look closer, and see in a different manner. As with any engaging act of architecture, this interest opens a dialogue with the aesthetics of the building as well as its broader environment.

At the Pulled Plaster House, spatial oscillation flips a voided negative courtyard space into a positive volume as a glazed-in terrarium. Again, one is asked to examine the structure closer, discover its shifts, and, in this case, to enter a dialogue on the legibility of changing figures.

Yet, when examining our other projects, we find more subtle gradations of readings, temporal shifts in the understanding of spatiality, materiality, and typology that open the possibility for users to engage an

Glitch House, Dominican Republic

Pulled Plaster House, New York, New York

architecture that is indeterminate. This happens through the creation of fluctuations that allow the nature of the spaces or materials we create to shift relative to the perception of the subject.

Whereas the material research at the Glitch House relies heavily upon the arrangement of the cement tiles on concrete masonry units to create an unexpected optical phenomenon, other projects have focused more directly on techniques of *making*—formation, fabrication, and manipulation—to break with expected readings of materiality. We look for intrinsic material possibilities and tweakable moments in the fabrication process to create tectonic ambiguities that contribute to the allure of the architecture.

At the Pulled Plaster House, the pulled plaster panels assemble to create a monolithic volume that is surprisingly soft and tactile. The sweeping geometry of the plaster is the result of a simple change to a traditional fabrication technique for crown moldings. At the Rock House, pick-hammering of the Twice-Baked Concrete mimics decades of erosion to reveal blue and green aggregate, but the patina of weathering is incongruent with the intentionality of the building's form and crisply excised crescent-shaped apertures. The formal legibility of the structure is understood simultaneously as a single mass eroded into six rocks and as disparate fragments that have been consciously arranged.

Here it is evident that our material research is uniquely biased by, as well as bound to, complex spatial investigations. To enter into dialogue with a material is to engage its spatial role within a building, to reveal how details or material relationships gather to

Rock House, Dominican Republic

Six Square House, Bridgehampton, New York

Retreat House, Dominican Republic

create a larger effect. Spatial oscillations therefore work in tandem with material research, as well as in the reverse. This is evident in projects both geometrically restrained and formally expressive.

At the Six Square House, the archetype of a gable roof house transforms as structural lines extend from one volume into another and result in a complex network of undulating ruled surfaces. The house's six masses read as autonomous from the exterior, while the interior ceilings flow continuously through a single connected space. In this example, the significance of typological oscillations is thoroughly examined in the context of vernacular references as well as construction conventions.

The Retreat House is perhaps our most dynamic project in terms of spatial complexity and transformations of a figure. The geometry of its meandering roof form and articulated structure are guided by parameters of cross ventilation, circulation, program, and landscape. Spatial oscillations exist in a more subtle manner through the orchestration of plan decisions and sectional shifts, allowing spaces to merge across unexpected view corridors, open corners, and shifting sectional floor plates. Any position within the retreat is loosely defined, facilitating connections among occupants and to the outside environment.

While both terms—oscillation and ambiguity—point in a similar direction, there are clear differences in their natures. Ambiguity encourages multiple subjective readings, while oscillation guides the eye or the mind along prescribed paths. And whereas ambiguity embraces fluidity, oscillation celebrates rigor and intentionality.

Perhaps the work itself bounces back and forth between these two terms. It may not be productive to lock it down under one summarizing term. Rather, the projects happily play on a tension between the undetermined and the determined, the open-ended and the rigorously analyzed.

Dominican Republic, 2019

Located on a lush, previously undeveloped site in the Dominican Republic, the Retreat House sits on the cusp of dense jungle to the south and pristine beach to the north. The 20,000-square-foot home is designed to take advantage of both faces of the property, drawing inspiration from the rich tropical landscape, sustainable design principles, and a diverse set of programmatic uses that focus on wellness and creative exchange.

Upon arrival, the Retreat House is gradually revealed on a meandering approach through the dense tropical foliage of the site. A sinuous foot-path of sand-set Lajas stones tracks through old-growth trees with a thick understory of Zamia palms dotted with tropical flowers. The building is first seen from a distance, the verticality of the weathered ipe siding slowly emerging through a field of silver tree trunks. The low slung, widespread mass of the house is never fully visible, but is pieced together from discrete vantage points along the path of approach.

The path through the forest is only the first step in a highly choreographed entry sequence that ultimately reveals the fundamental massing parti of the building. The initial vignettes seen from the trees suggest the upper level of the house as a hovering, wood-clad volume gently undulating in section above the sloping ground plane while also veering in plan to curl around trees. The floating wood volume is thick and immense; openings in the facade read as voids and carvings, and the continuous material application of silvered ipe rainscreen cladding wraps the roof, walls, and underside into a single, taut skin.

Downspouts: vegetation climbs the ethereal stainless steel expanded metal mesh down-spouts, which delicately spiral water down during even extreme rain events.

Upon nearing the entry to the house, however, the initial reading of a hovering building is promptly subverted. The seemingly autonomous mass rests on concrete planes that are thoughtfully positioned but exhibit none of the formal dexterity of the wood facades. The ipe battens of the upper level idiosyncratically drop all the way down to grade, bypassing the concrete base to create a stable foot.

The massive nature of the building peels apart into a cascading series of nested arcs on the edges of the roof, on the intermediate floor slab, and on the wall of the foot, temporarily revealing a language of strips and surfaces that unravels from the mass of the upper level before neatly realigning and continuing on with business as usual. This moment of oscillating languages knitted together by tightly resolved geometries hints at the rich ambiguity and layering of figures that exist throughout the building. At moments the house is singular and monolithic, and at other moments the house is a series of related radial arcs, planar in nature.

The true moment of entrance to the Retreat House begins with a sense of extreme compression, as visitors pass beneath a 70-foot span set a mere 8 feet off the ground. This compression releases upward into a courtyard defined by textured white concrete walls around a magnificent Ficus tree dripping with orchids. The courtyard slopes up steeply along the central path, and a carefully incised opening in the concrete walls frames a direct view through the house and to the ocean beyond. The sense of arrival is tied into the data of landscape, section, and horizon.

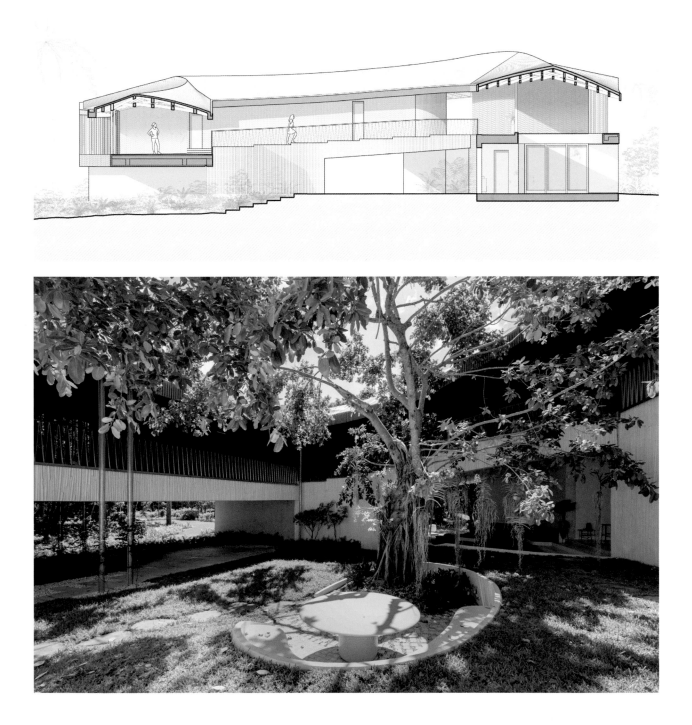

The courtyard is not a center in terms of occupation for guests to the Retreat. Rather, the courtyard and its magnificent ficus tree are an anchor point that counterbalances the patio and pool to the north. Spanning between these two points (courtyard and patio) is the open-air, double-height living room, which functions programmatically as the hub and gathering moment.

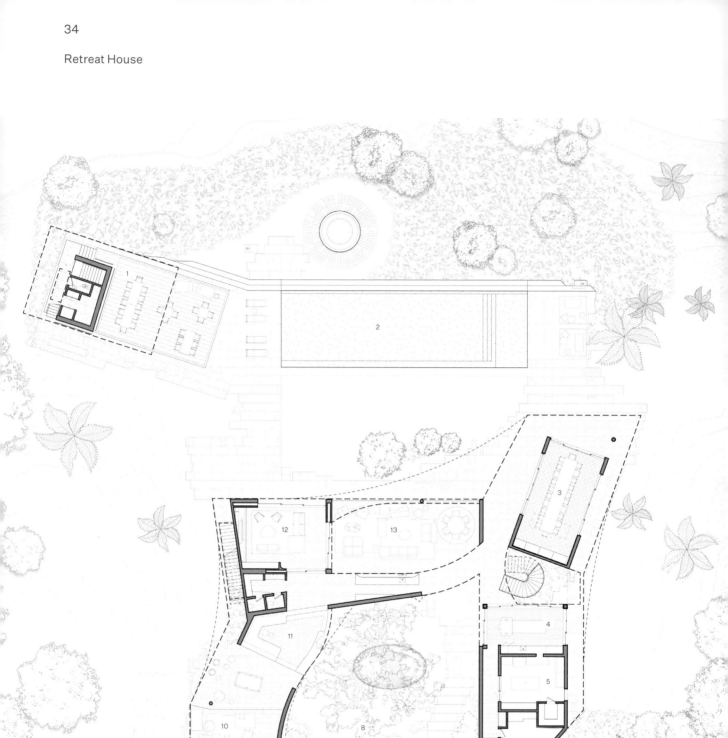

Befitting a building so thoroughly embedded in dense tropical foliage as the Retreat House, the most legibly sculptural aspect of the architecture is displayed internally in the fluttering assemblage of scissor trusses that structures the roof. It is here that the concepts of the building are most explicitly articulated; rhythm and orientation describe a courtyard parti, as sectional undulations expose both top and bottom, inside and outside of a geometrically rich surface providing rain protection, shading, ventilation, and organization.

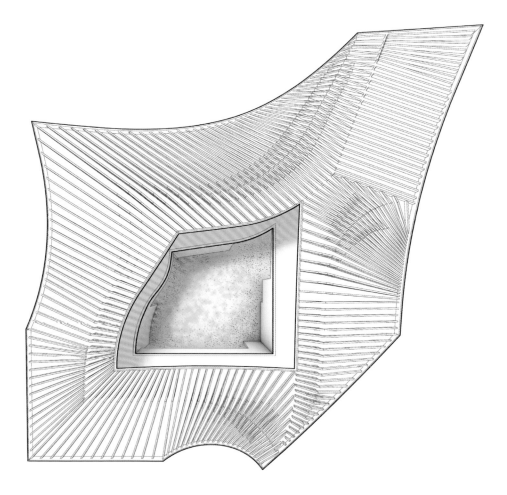

The figure of the roof itself comprises 160 unique scissor trusses, jack trusses, and rafters supported by slender mahogany columns and sculpted curving beams. The repetitive aggregation of straight truss members as a group implies a series of ruled surfaces that are geometrically dynamic but ultimately agreeable to the physical parameters of timber and sheet materials necessary for cladding and finishing. Less visible is the complex engineering of both the individual members and the overall roof assembly into a rigid diaphragm capable of sustaining large, sail-like expanses of heavy timber roof in an environment where extreme hurricanes and seismic events are primary design considerations. A thickened zone of structural timber chords and collectors runs above the exposed trusses and beneath the ipe batten rainscreen roof finish to yield a surprisingly simple and beautiful assembly.

At an individual level, each truss is a carefully designed and artfully fabricated element. Joinery and fasteners were thoroughly considered for a tectonic clarity of assembly. Complex three-dimensional joints were fabricated using computer numerical control (CNC) milling, the top surfaces of each member were sculpted to allow sheathing to flow smoothly across the sloping roof. The entire roof assembly was pre-fitted in fabrication prior to delivery to the site, allowing for a rapid erection process with a minimum of field adjustments.

The spatiality and figure of the roof are prescribed to both performance and occupation of the building, shifting to establish a sequential spatial logic relative to how you engage the exterior. The undulating surfaces of the roof generally comprise a ring surrounding the center court of the building, with the outer edges gently swooping to shepherd the footprint of the building around trees and other site features and toward the spectacular views of both ocean and forest. The boundaries of the roof hold an alternating series of mahogany-clad volumes (containing bedrooms) and open-air lounges that bleed off the courtyard corridor and correspond to moments of vertical circulation (stairs).

Retreat House

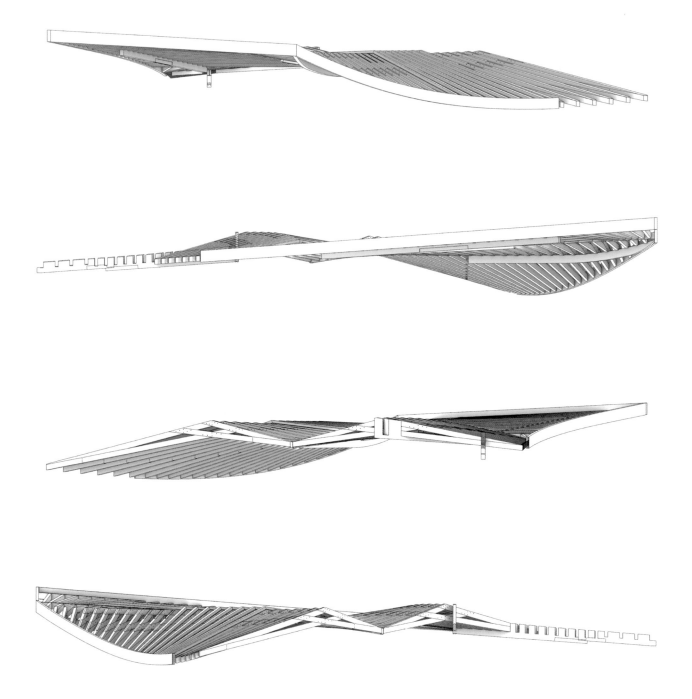

Roof structure: the undulating form of the roof
is approximated by a series of scissor trusses,
jack trusses, rafters, and beams that flatten and
steepen in response to support conditions, program, and ventilation needs of the spaces below.

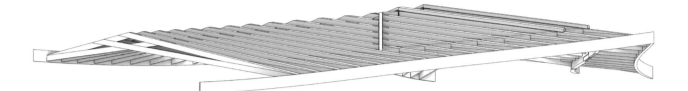

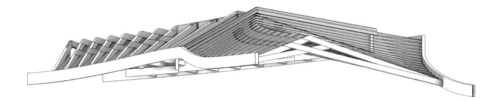

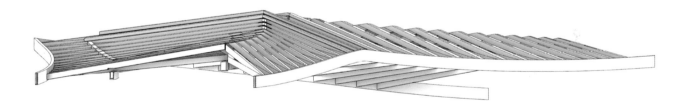

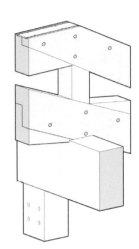

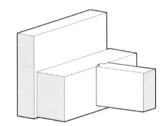

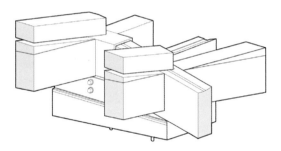

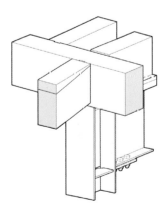

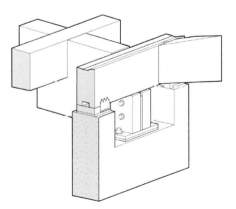

Joinery details: the complex geometry of the roof
trusses, beams, and columns is reconciled in a
series of connections that reference traditional
timber joinery methods while integrating highly
performative steel structural elements.

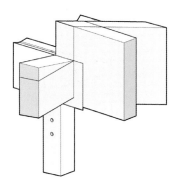

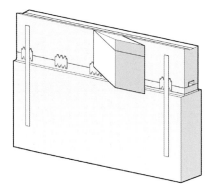

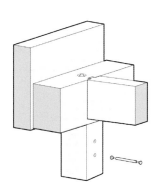

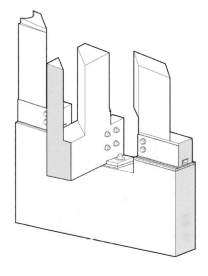

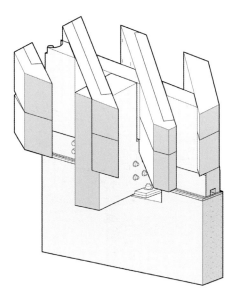

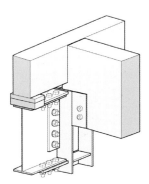

Guest bedroom: The ridgeline is at its peak along the back walls of the bedroom suites.

Guest bathroom: En-suite bathrooms include custom designed cement tiles fabricated in the Dominican Republic and cast concrete vanities.

Interiors: the design and material palette of the interiors relied heavily on airy, neutral textiles contrasted with tactile natural materials and moments of vibrant color.

At the demising walls to the bedrooms, the ridgeline of the roof sits directly above the structural spine wall separating corridor from dormitory, and the trusses defining the roof slope are steeply peaked. This typical gabled roof condition has performative benefits for the bedrooms—low eaves limit solar heat gain, while high ceilings at the spine wall passively vent hot air and induce natural ventilation from the operable glass doors of each room. The ridgeline breaks from this geometric logic at each open-air lounge, curling out perpendicular to the outer exterior roof edge. Simultaneously, the steep gable of the truss sections lowers and flattens out, creating tunnel-like spaces tuned for cross ventilation and open both to the court-yard and exterior facade. This formal flourish puts the most dramatic and performative moments of assembly on full display in spaces used for gatherings, games, and lounging.

The courtyard stands separate from the other gray concrete planes that line the ground floor of the building in both its pristine white finish as well as its dramatically textured surface. "Palmcrete" defines the walls of the courtyard not as exterior surfaces of the masses it surrounds, but as forming a distinct internal room of its own. It is a singular figure.

The development of the palmcrete was opportunistic in nature, one of many happy accidents—especially as they inspire material experiments— outlined in this book. Several iterations of form liners and other embedded casting techniques were studied before realizing that the stem (petiole and rachis) of palm fronds—abundant in the surrounding jungle land- scape—could be stripped to leave an elongated, tapering, convex slat with a nearly perfect shape and texture for releasing from site-cast concrete.

The flexible nature of the palm segments allowed them to be tightly packed against one another, bent and curved to accommodate irregularities of length and width from stem to stem. The process of packing the palms onto the formwork was loosely controlled to maintain a general verticality, but we explicitly encouraged drift and shifting patterns of flow rather than striving for parallel patterning.

The white concrete was carefully specified to maximize its bright color and hyper-smooth texture. While concrete was used throughout the Retreat House to emphasize sculptural artisanal elements (the site-cast concrete bar, the elliptical courtyard bench, and built-in furniture throughout), the deployment of this material on the monumental courtyard walls marks the significance of this space in occupancy as well as its fundamental role in the architectural organization of the building. The walls were cast in single pours and without formwork joints or form ties marring either the inward palmcrete or the perfectly abstract smooth walls that face outward to the surrounding rooms.

Sitting quietly in the dense foliage behind the Retreat House is another building shaped by the site's spectacular trees, albeit in a very different manner. Significantly smaller in scale than the Retreat House, the Guest House is a four-bedroom accommodation. On the edge of the largest naturally occurring clearing on the 4.5-acre site and slightly removed from the shade of the dense jungle canopy, the Guest House receives plenty of direct sunlight and cooling breezes. The bedrooms can be converted into studios or other workspaces, providing the opportunity for artist or writer residencies on the property.

The organizational principles of the Guest House are simple: each of the four identical suites are oriented to face one of two magnificent old-growth Ficus trees on the far edge of the clearing. The suites are spaced apart to create shared outdoor porch areas, yet the entirety of the structure is unified under a single arcing roof. By alternating which of the two trees each suite faces, the view direction varies from room to room and provides each guest mutual visual privacy from their neighbors. The suites are further grouped into two pairs, each sharing an open breezeway entry porch, and the two pairs are separated by an outdoor living room with built-in seating and a hanging wicker chair looking out toward the gardens.

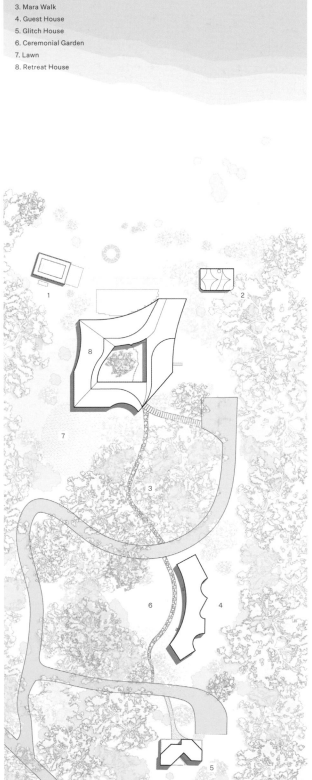

1. Yoga Pavilion
2. Rock House
3. Mara Walk
4. Guest House
5. Glitch House
6. Ceremonial Garden
7. Lawn
8. Retreat House

The suites are efficient in layout and are designed to maximize connections with the exterior. Full-wall sliding glass doors comprise both the front and back elevations of each suite, dramatically framing the Ficus trees from the bedrooms and opening up the bathrooms to the more intimately scaled tropical gardens behind the Guest House. These operable window walls are also crucial for completely opening the building to east-west cross ventilation as well as creating a direct connection between the sitting areas within the bedrooms and the front porch spaces directly adjacent.

Like the Retreat House, the Guest House is located above the storm surge flood level of the site. To raise the vantage point from which visitors to the Guest House view the surrounding gardens, the earth is mounded up to the building, rather than placing the habitable areas on a second floor or elevating the entire building on pilotis. These mounds become an integral feature of the gardens (and of the overall spatial experience) by providing a canvas for a brightly colored arcing plant bed that follows the roofline on the front of the building, and smaller, more discrete mounds that define the gardens and provide spatial separation and visual privacy to the bathrooms on the rear of the building.

Unifying the four suites under a single roof serves an important role in mediating the building's spatial relationship to the site. Although the envelope of each individual suite is orthogonal and discrete, its sloping ceiling extends beyond the footprints of enclosure and collides with the other roofs to create a faceted and irregular ceiling scape. On the front of the building, this ceiling scape is cropped by a single arc centered on the sunny clearing in the adjacent landscape. This singular gesture reinforces the building's orientation toward the garden and creates an interesting figure on the roof fascia.

As the sloping suite ceilings hit the fascia at different heights and orientations, a subtle geometry emerges; by setting this undulating ceiling edge against a level, horizontal line capping the roof, the variation in the ceiling heights is made more explicit and is registered in elongated, tapering forms across the fascia.

On the rear of the building, the entry breezeways and the outdoor living room are sharply cropped by scoops into the building. In conjunction with the immaterially abstract stucco of the walls, floors, and ceilings of these spaces, the unexpected geometry creates a fish-eye view of the gardens beyond, flattening them in a surprising cinematic moment of optical effect.

The Glitch House rests within a natural clearing just south of the Retreat House and the Guest House. The house is carefully sited, taking into account the angle of the sun, and oriented both to facilitate comfortable habitation and to amplify the range of dynamic aesthetic effects visible on the building's colorful skin throughout the day. Along the north edge of the house, a roof garden offers a shaded area for occupants to relax and dine under the trees. From the roof garden, inhabitants are lifted to an elevation in which the ocean becomes visible and breezes flow.

The ground floor of the house contains areas for retreat storage, landscaping equipment, maintenance parking, and a laundry facility, while the upper floor of the building contains the bedrooms and living spaces, elevated above the 100-year flood level of the site.

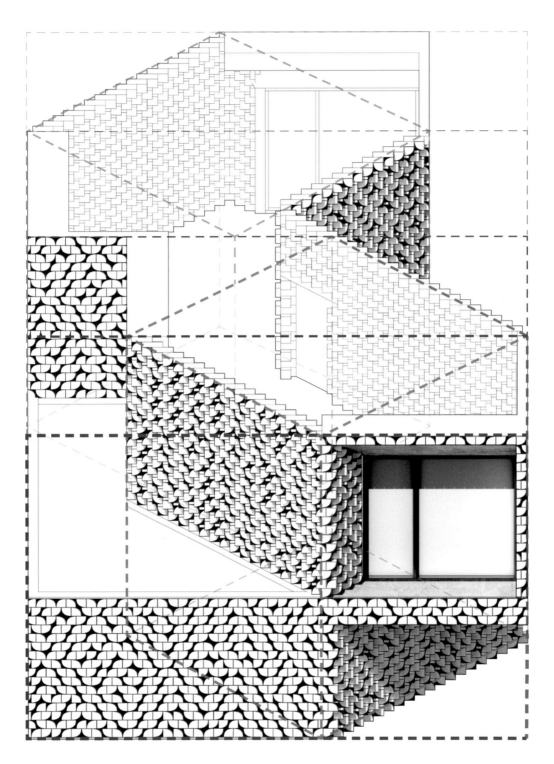

The chamfered corners of the upper level align vertically at a near mid-point of the elevations below, suggesting a rotated geometry in which nearly platonic cubes are intersected between the two levels. The layout of the CMU blocks on the facades of the chamfered walls follows the orthogonal geometry from above/below, resulting in highly agitated surfaces.

The large windows in each living area maintain an immediate connection with the exterior environment, giving the sense that guests are occupying a treehouse or nest. The interiors contain Dominican-fabricated rattan armoires, handwoven wicker chairs, jute rugs, and colorful linens.

1. Terrace
2. Bedroom
3. Green Roof
4. Bath
5. Living/Dining Room

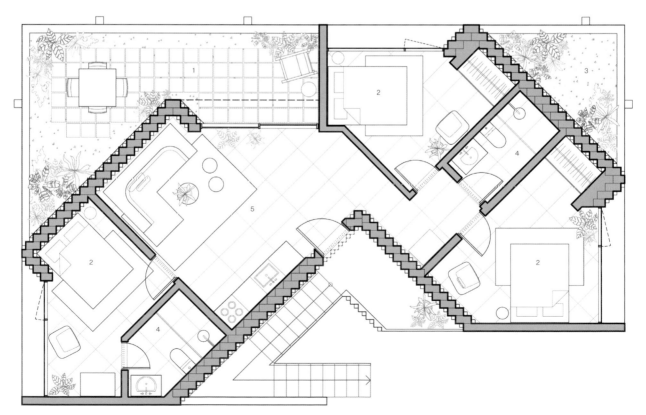

The initial experience of the exterior is uncanny. The building compels visitors to look closer, move around it, and enter into a dialogue with its materiality, spatiality, and broader environment. Yet, the project is incredibly simple, powerful though a DIY sensibility that is didactically expressed from conception to execution, like LEGO bricks with colorful decals.

The house first appears as an impenetrable monolithic folly without windows or doors. The colors and pattern of the encaustic cement tiles simultaneously embed the mass in the surrounding landscape and emphasize the corners and edges of its own geometry. At moments, the house reads as a backdrop attempting to dissolve into the tropical foliage. At other moments it exaggerates its figure, reversing the frame and using the jungle as a natural backdrop. This oscillation of figure is the result of the calibration of pattern and color of the cement tiles relative to the boundaries of each facade.

The exterior envelope of the otherwise orthogonal building is truncated at the corners to shape triangular voids that precisely alternate from lower level to upper (and back) around the perimeter of the house. These diagonal shifts between floors create horizontal slippages in the building's massing that manifest as cantilevered overhangs providing areas of shade on the ground floor while carving out occupiable roof decks for the living spaces on the upper floor.

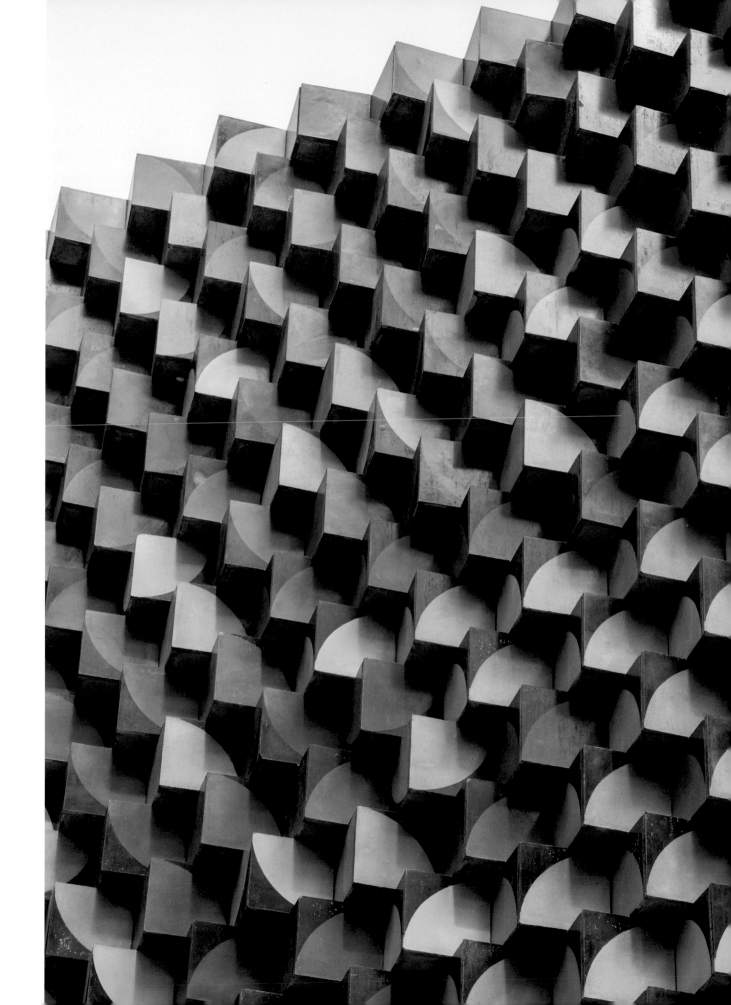

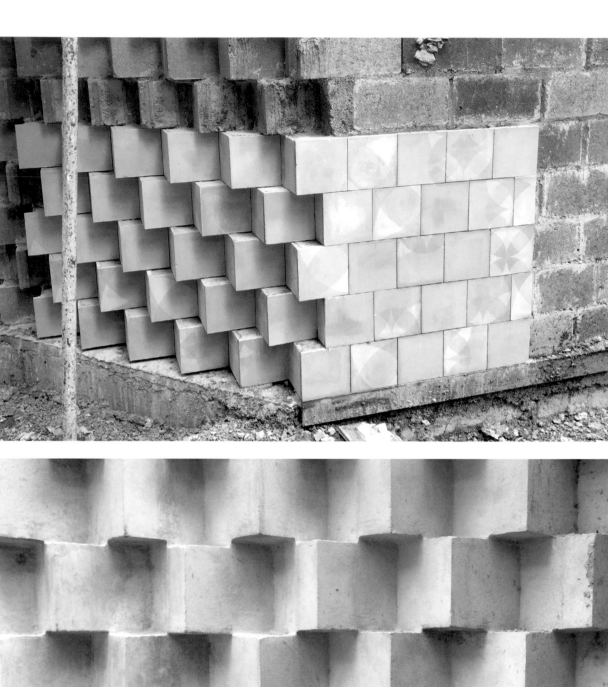

The cladding of the facades is the result of fortuitous dimensional standards. Staggering the 8 × 8 × 16 inch concrete masonry units (CMU) across the chamfered facades exposed naked 8 × 8 inch faces, which perfectly correspond to the standard dimensions of the artisanal cement tiles ubiquitous in the Dominican Republic.

The coloration and layout of the more than ten thousand encaustic cement tiles are far from arbitrary. Every tile was intentionally positioned to create fluctuating readings across the building's skin. The pattern on the flat walls tends to be more intricate and repetitive, developing over arrangements of seven to ten adjacent tiles. The chamfered walls, which shift in and out along the surface, have much simpler patterns but are animated by the shadows cast by the offset zigzagging CMU one course above or below. The graphics transition slowly and seamlessly across the facade, with a scattered quality in the center of walls coalescing into more unified, monolithic aggregation at the building's edges and corners.

Each square tile contains a quarter-circle arc pattern, and either the inside or outside of this arc is shaded black. The arc was selected to contrast the intensely repetitive cubic geometry on the chamfered facades. It introduces a curvilinear graphic component that begins to resist the overwhelming orthogonality of the physical structure to suggest curving modules rather than rectilinear bricks. The arc pattern also crucially subdivides each tile into two unequal areas, inside and outside, creating the opportunity to tune graphic density across the facades in a way that other equal-area delineations (for instance, a corner-to-corner diagonal) could not. Oscillating the black-filled area of the arc allows for an unexpected and extended exercise in pattern recognition through the gathering and separating of pattern, tone, contrast, and color.

Crescent pattern 7A on a flat surface

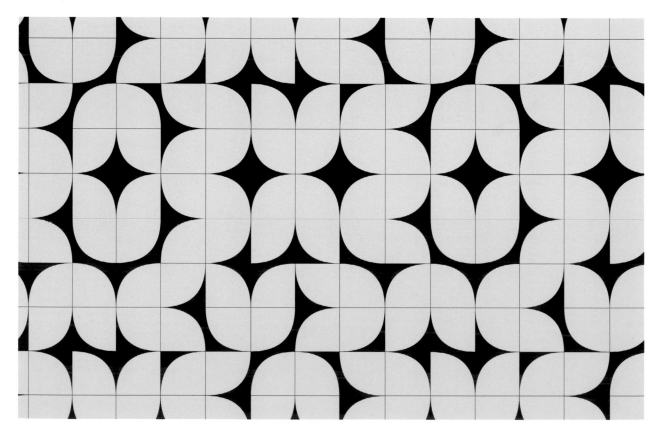

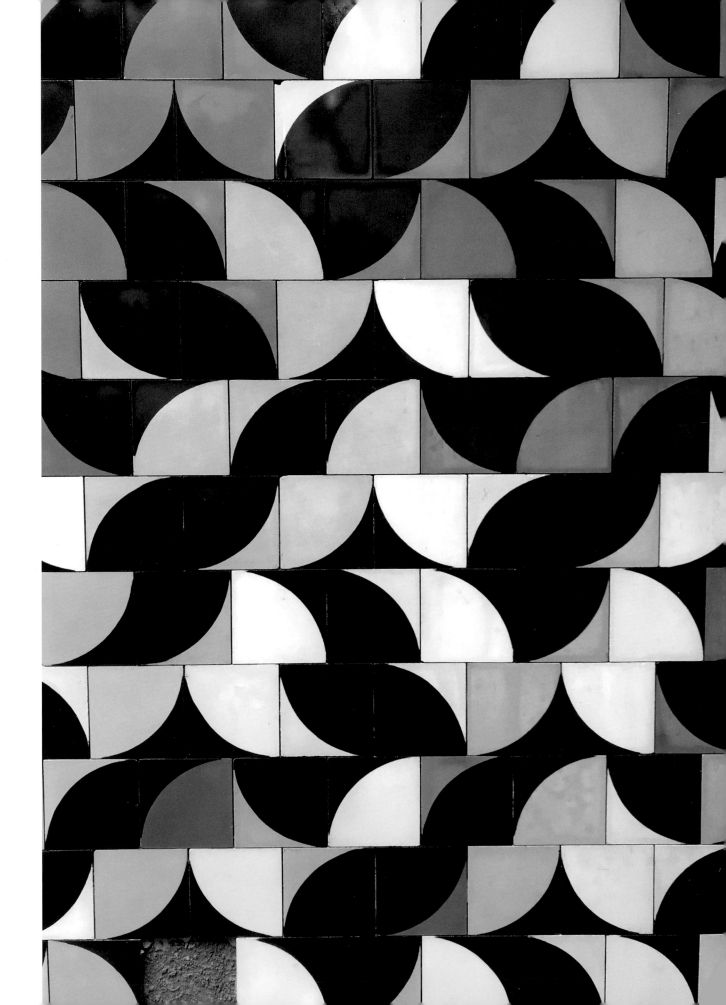

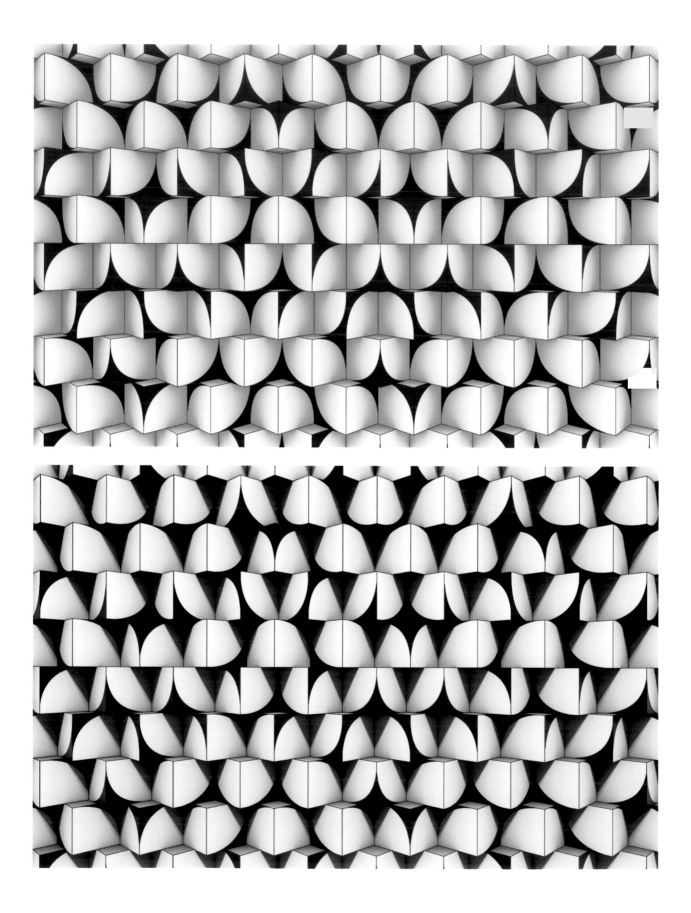

The patterns on *flat* facades often mirror and rotate the tiles in a decorative and floral manner, creating motifs that suggest petals, whales, worms, and Pac-Man. However, applied to the *staggered* CMU facades, the same patterning transforms dramatically as shadows formed below the coursing of offset blocks become entangled with the graphics of the aggregated tiles. The legibility of the pattern is confused, and the facade becomes fuzzy as the patterns gradually transition across the surface. The shadows can be soft and gauzy, harsh and defined, triangular, rectangular, square, or amorphic.

While the bold black arcs on the tiles are central to the graphic character of each elevation, the addition of color further defamiliarizes the building. Shifting gradients of yellow, green, blue, and purple bleed from tile to tile and weave a continuous underlayer distinct from the staccato of the black arcs. From far away, the building reads as having a soft turquoise tint, a glitchy smudge within the jungle landscape.

Crescent pattern 7A on a undulating/chamfered surface

Crescent pattern 7A on a undulating/chamfered surface with strong fall shadows

The sensibilities for the project are somewhere between Q*bert and the chromatophores of reptiles and mollusks. The intentionally diagrammatic "blocky-ness" gives way to flowing murmuration of graded color tones and textures. One's ability to oscillate between these visuals readings is as simple as to squint an eye.

Crescent pattern 7A on a undulating/chamfered surface with strong fall shadows and color

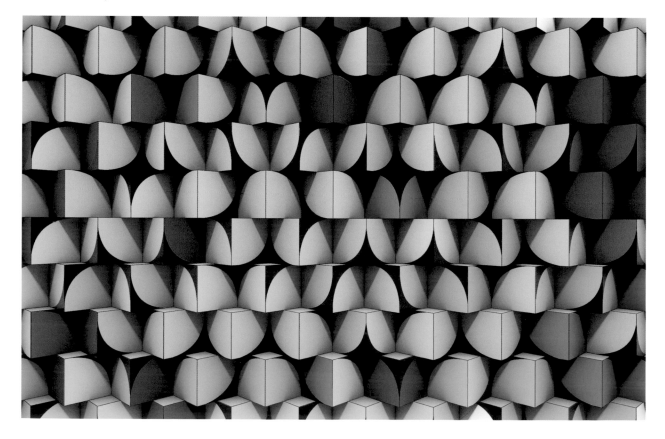

Glitch House

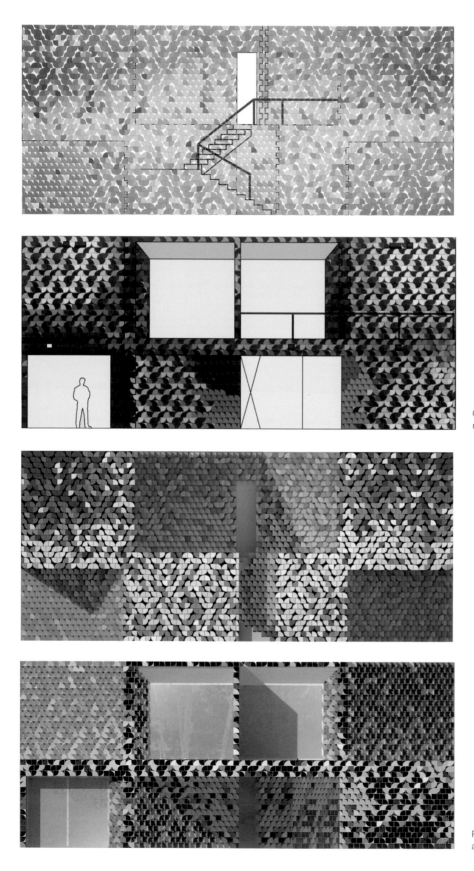

Concept pattern and color studies,
north and south elevations

Final pattern and color, north
and south elevations

The Carraig Ridge Fireplace is a folly, a communal pavilion on a 650-acre development of 44 contemporary rural retreats located approximately 80 kilometers west of Calgary in the foothills of the Rocky Mountains. The structure enshrouds the conventional fire pit to create a habitable fireplace that can be used as a gathering spot throughout the year; it is a hearth to the adjacent Lake Anna and surrounding hills.

Although predating the Glitch House by a few years, the Carraig Ridge Fireplace similarly required development of a straightforward method of construction using readily available materials. As such, the fireplace is constructed of stacked Douglas fir heavy timber cut into lengths of three to five feet and placed into one of six unique planimetric positions subtly twisting around an implied center. This loose interpretation of stacked firewood produces a thick yet porous veil that simultaneously shapes a prismatic exterior and cylindrical interior.

The gaps between timbers allow moments of oblique views back to the landscape and a soft, lantern glow when a fire is lit within. There are two distinct apertures carved through the thick poché of the stacked timbers: a corner entry and a framed view to the lake. From both interior and exterior, the articulation of the four facades and shifting porosity encourages visitors to move around and within the humble shelter.

Alberta, Canada, 2014

The fireplace utilizes stacked coursing and rotation from level to level to create thick and agitated facades—conceptually akin to the chamfered facades of the Glitch House. Both projects also generate an ambiguity of figure through pixelization. Like the Glitch House, the Carraig Ridge Fireplace is a glinting smudge mark when seen from afar, while up close it is a simple and even crude exercise in stacking.

Because of the fireplace's rotated geometry, each piece of the stacked wood displays its solar orientation and the duration of its exposure to sun through its specific weathering. A gradual tonal gradient reveals itself over time, adding depth to the interwoven structure.

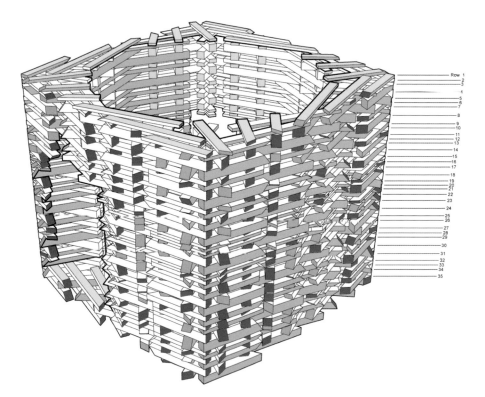

Bryan Young   There are many interesting elements to your work and how you think as an artist that overlay with Young Projects' architecture. I see in your work quite often an aesthetic association with characteristics of natural environments—whether it's biological or maybe geological, moss or plant life or different kinds of organic formations and related tectonics. What you're trying to tease out of your textiles, from an aesthetic perspective, seems to have associations with the way elements tend to form naturally.

Dana Barnes   Yeah, that is it exactly. Typically my work is informed by the gritty central beauty of natural forces. Works like *Endolith Cast* are taken from lichen growth colonizing within rock formations and sprouting out into intricate spurs of vivid color patches. I also can be inspired by experimenting with materials and processes, just what might dominate my way of thinking at a particular time. I like to think of my work as an approach to sculpting with texture; each work has a dense tactile quality and exhibits some sort of dimensionality that is atypical of textile art.

I'm also inspired by my travels. In March 2020, we showed at the Park Avenue Armory a piece called *A'ā Sculpted Mass*, which was inspired by the jagged earth, lava rocks, and formations of Iceland. The piece is very dense and sculptural in its makeup. It hung on the wall, but at the base, it spills into a form onto the floor. In making it, we studied color, especially the black, to evoke the way the light would hit the rocks in Iceland. We experimented with adding an oxidized gold leaf into the textile. It was truly a study of how light reacts in nature and how we could bring that to life in textual form and in a gallery setting.

Bryan Young   There is an interesting tension that arises between inspirations from nature, from which you're starting to cultivate an idea or direction for a piece, and the aesthetics that emerge through the actual material properties and forces that are being applied, as you say, by experimenting with materials and processes. For example, the degree to which a weave becomes dense, the degree to which different strands bundle together, and the grains and structure of the material all contribute to formation in a manner that is maybe more materially direct than the initial references; it's as if there are intricate, almost unknowable properties that you're starting to display in order to provide momentum in parallel to the references of nature.

I see something similar in some of our buildings, preciously because there's a kind of sequential study of material actions and material forces. At the Glitch House, it's not until we started to have a critical mass of materiality and geometry that we discovered potential relationships of colors, textures, and pattern. Yet the aesthetic origins for the facade reference camouflage patterns and reptile skin. Maybe this is part of the allure of our related projects, the manner in which there are recognizable references on the one hand, yet unfamiliar resolution due to the ways material empirically behaves through a set of highly charged forces, sometimes maybe intentional and sometimes random.

I'm curious to maybe hear a bit more about your process, about moments when you pull back and let the materials dictate tactility, density, and the sculptural quality, and then other moments when you jump back in and you begin to tweak it a certain way to some curated direction.

Dana Barnes   It's just all a balance of form and technique, and trial and error. It can be haphazard and unstudied. It evolves organically, but we have to have some control. I'm constantly jumping in to tweak it. The mistakes are usually the best part of it, though. That's why the humble, raw qualities of wool are interesting to me as a medium; I can manipulate and contort it through non-formulaic techniques of looping, knotting, twisting, and

Glitch House, Dominican Republic, 2018

Dana Barnes, *A'ā Sculpted Mass*, 2020, Merino, yak, Gotland, and Leicester wools; silk, bamboo, hemp, and flax fibers; and oxidized 18K gold.

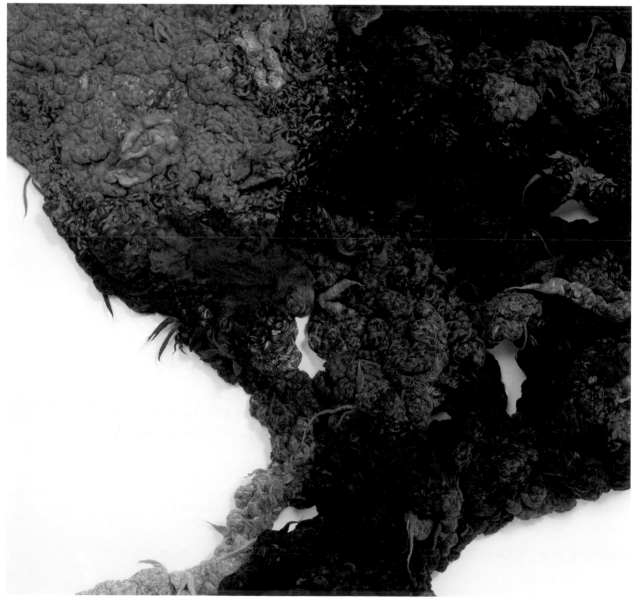

braiding, and then, by employing the boiling process, these odd and unexpected organic abstractions are formed.

Before we added the gold leaf to *A´ā*, we had experimented with oxidation and studied how it might occur as it would in the volcanic extrusion process from which it was inspired. It needed to look like part of Earth's crust, not just appear as a gold bling moment.

The intention was to bring all the fragments together in a way that spoke to shades of color as well as to being alive. This is the other common thread through most of the work: to convey a sense of aliveness through some sort of flow or movement.

Bryan Young   Your description of the mistakes and the accidents really resonates with me. In our material and prototyping experiments, we're often trying to find something within a technique of making that breaks its own methodology. Sometimes it's intentional and sometimes randomness comes into play. Those are the "happy accidents" that lead to an unexpected aesthetic quality.

In the Glitch House, light and shadow begin to interact with the surface based on solar orientation. Through a series of studies in the studio, we realized that the manner in which you would see the graphic pattern of the tiles would change significantly depending upon the angle of the sun and the shadows it casts. The shadows become entangled with the graphics of the tile itself. And in that sense, the facades almost feel alive; you can perceive a subtle vibration. The visual associations may be abstract and geometric, where you confuse some of the graphics of the tiles as shadows, or the associations can be natural—are these fluttering leaves in the jungle?

In developing the facade, at times we inserted brighter colors, not just to have a pop of color, but because we realized that if the surface is too monotonous, you lose that quality of movement.

Dana Barnes   Are there any patterns that repeat?

Bryan Young   On certain facades you do see elements or groupings that repeat, like a motif. These areas may feel more graphically artificial, almost

Dana Barnes, *RETOLD: Mahal Blue Field*, 2017, Merino wool and silk fibers.

Dana Barnes, *RETOLD: Bidjar Iron*, 2017, Merino wool, silk and bamboo fibers

like a wallpaper, but as the pattern stops repeating, it increasingly feels more random and more natural, at least in the manner in which we are using the word "natural" in this conversation.

At the Glitch House the pattern also shifts to emphasize a boundary or an edge or a center. In your art, you seem to add color or other accentuating scales and textures to talk about boundaries or different zones of articulation within the piece itself.

> Dana Barnes   In *A'ā*, there was too much of a contrast from the blue to the black at first. The colors didn't seem to coexist naturally, so we created fragments to gradually merge the flow of color. We call these "fusion pieces" in which we layer and knot gradient fiber colors together in a painterly fashion to articulate color transition as it would occur in nature. Many of the artists in my studio are painters, so this process to them is like blending oil paints. With the neutral color that we inserted beside the black at the bottom of the piece, the decision was quite different. There we liked the graphic contrast. It's just like in the Glitch House, where you have certain lines that you want to highlight and others that you want to blend.

Bryan Young   When you talk about blurring and fusing and achieving a painterly quality, I also think about your *RETOLD* series, in which you use intricately hand-knotted Persian carpets as a substrate for layering and infusing wool. At times the original tapestry is clearly legible, but where exactly your intervention occurs blurs so interestingly with the existing colors and the existing narrative of a found object, so to speak. There's a fusion of the background and the foreground.

> Dana Barnes   Pat Passlof, an abstract expressionist painter who previously worked in my studio space, left some antique Persian rugs that I began to study and find fascinating. Each comprised its own unique story with motifs interwoven reflecting the regions where it was created. They embodied so much tradition and utilized the same medium of my practice, wool. I wanted to study the contrast between the highly structured Persian

carpet and applications of wool as it is used in my practice, which is unstructured, abstract, and organic.

I also became interested in abstract painting and by extension the actual textural oil paint clots that were left on the floor of my studio from the days of Pat painting here. I began a process of layering vibrant wool fiber plumes onto the Persian substrate sort of like the ductus of a painter's palette knife and brush on a canvas. This articulated movement and texture of clotted, caked, sculptural surfaces brought dimensionality to the antique rugs. This process was further realized by needle-fusing the fibers into the Persian rugs and wet-bonding the wools together.

Bryan Young   Mediating between structured and unstructured, abstract, and organic conditions is another theme at the Glitch House. The facade areas with repeating motifs could be considered the structured zones, and the introduction of coloration the organic and flowing zones.

While this work is perhaps less inspired by nature directly, I look at *RETOLD* and think of aging and weathering, growth patterns of decay. In certain areas, the layering of fibers leads to knots that almost look like mold formations, and the white fibers have a streaking pattern similar to cobwebs. It seems that there's a process that begins to take the aesthetics of the Persian rug and blur them into abstraction, while it is still influenced by a system of hierarchy and formation.

There also seems to be a fiction that you're creating in the work, which I would relate to the design of Young Project's Rock House. The house utilizes poured white concrete with an aggregate of broken-up blue and green concrete, which we then exposed through a process of sandblasting. The concrete finish appears to have weathered, yet this sensation sits at odds with an underlying condition that is the precision of the geometry of the structure. Similar to the *RETOLD* series, it has multiple acts.

When you are making these fictions on a material level, they don't actually have to obey the way materials might behave or respond in seemingly natural conditions; you can construct new behaviors or incongruent associations. Again, at the Rock House, the surface may seem as if it's eroding, yet at the same time, there is incredible crispness to its geometry and incisions.

Dana Barnes, *RETOLD: Tekke Madder*, 2017,
Merino wool, silk and bamboo fibers.

Effortless, But It's Not

Dana Barnes, *CLING* installation, 2016, Merino, Leicester, Gotland, Icelandic wools; silk and bamboo fibers.

In the *RETOLD* Persian, one can clearly see act 1, the pattern of the rug, and the departure to act 2, your interwoven and overlaid process; but at the same time these parts have somehow become inseparable through the sensitivity to grain, color, and texture.

> Dana Barnes   Exactly. And in fact, the momentum is often uncontrollable. The material we work with here in the studio is fused together through a wet-bonding process. That's when it takes on a form of its own; it can create something more fabulous, or it can overboil and be a dud. We never throw anything away—we repurpose it somehow if it's not particularly right for what we were aiming for in a specific work. But very often we can't control its end result through the bonding process.
> We call this the "organic gesture." A work like *Cling* was completely led by the material itself. We experimented with a lot of new fibers, and we didn't know how they would take the boiling process or the felting process that we custom developed in our studio. In terms of the spontaneity of the hand and the material, you just have to go with it and let the material evolve into its own form and celebrate that character.

Bryan Young   For a competition for the New York art institution The Kitchen, we did a series of plaster casts using furniture upholstery and bent pencil rods for the mold. You can't make the pencil rod or related bulging of the mold's foam do anything you want it to do; there are only certain ways and figures in which you can bend this rod due to its own thickness and rigidity and the foam's cellular density. There are tendencies in which the foam wants to move away from the rods. These contingent material reactions are not planned and therefore lead to a language and form in the final cast that feels oddly undesigned.
The gestures that exist within the topography of the surface of the plaster cast requires an artisan and a unique materially contingent process of transformation. This may be similar in concept to your description of boiling; we don't know exactly what we're going to get until we cast it.

Dana Barnes   We definitely do start with some sort of idea, but the fibers can be unyielding. We try to custom formulate the wet-bonding process, kind of like creating a recipe, in the hope of repeating a specific technique. But the recipes never have consistent results because the material always does its own thing.

Everything we make in the studio is handmade, and the result is not unlike how structures evolve organically in nature.

Bryan Young   In architecture, we're often trying to control a design process, especially as technology has allowed an architect to predetermine many of the physical components of a project. Taken to an extreme, building today is more about assembling unique pieces rather than crafting, which is more transformative in essence.

We do experiments—sometimes just within our office at the scale of something we can build by hand, but also in metal foundries or woodshops, working with material artisans—so that we can create a productive road bump within this trajectory of trying to control the design process. For us, that road bump is often a material that wants to behave in a manner that we can't dictate. The result is much more complex than anything that we could intentionally design on our own.

I see something similar in a lot of your work, but especially in *Cling*—the way the knots want to hang, where formations of knots begin to kind of bundle, how that works with gravity and momentum. And, at a certain point, some strands can begin to break off, and, at other moments, strands feel like they want to group back together. And I suspect those are relationships that you might sketch out, but when you actually start making it might go in a different direction.

Dana Barnes   We often start with a sketch, but I always have to tell clients that this is an organic process and the final work is not going to look exactly like the sketch. The colors will be as we determine them to be from the outset, but where the color happens in the work and what organic shape emerges may not appear precisely like in the sketch. Honestly, the most compelling aspects of the piece usually happen unintentionally.

Bryan Young   In our material experiments, it's not until we do a full-scale mock-up, or even up until we finish a building, that we really know how these elements are going to behave. We're going to start a second Glitch House based upon the observations we've made in the first house. It is a scale of iteration that is very rare in architecture, and we are extremely fortunate to have the opportunity.

Dana Barnes   I used to fight that quite a bit. I thought only one or two of a certain idea or development should exist. I had to learn to appreciate the idea that a series is okay, because each artwork is unique anyway.

In the studio, we encourage artisans to push the boundaries of spontaneity, anti-pattern, irregularity, and non-formulaic gestures, but at the end of the day we aim to have some sort of structure and deliberate flow to maintain quality and material attributes that are representative of the studio. So I hope that it looks effortless, but it's not.

In most of the works, there's a studied effort to the way we swell the material in areas to distort it into amorphous shapes, for example. And there's training involved for the artisans that are new to the studio. Even though I always want to foster a free and unforced approach to gestural knotting techniques, at the same time the work should be beautiful and have constraint to some degree.

Bryan Young   There's a sensitive and masterly artistry between what is designed, curated, and intentionally created and the material principles that are, to some extent—out of our control, aesthetics that relate to scale, formation, and, maybe most significantly, the negotiation between materials and techniques. What may then ultimately encapsulate both your work and ours is precisely what you just said: "It looks effortless, but it's not."

New York, 2015

At the Pulled Plaster House, the spatial narrative focuses upon shifting readings of solid and void in the project's section. In this duplex unit occupying the thirteenth and fourteenth floors and the roof of a historic building in New York's Tribeca neighborhood, an initial cut through the roof opens the interior of the floor plates to light, air, and landscape. Upon arriving to the house—which in this case means exiting an elevator on the fourteenth floor—one immediately and unexpectedly encounters an exterior courtyard space open to the sky.

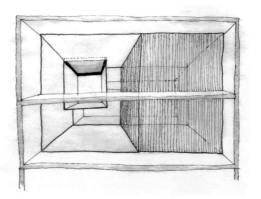

The opening cut through the roof is clad in black and glazed with expansive glass panels set in black metal frames. The inside face of the existing exterior wall is similarly black, suggesting an inverted, reflective prism hollowed out from the historic building mass. Vegetation spills over from the roof above and sprouts from the floor of the courtyard. This glassy court dramatically contrasts the thick masonry envelope with arched tripartite windows and creates an improbable sanctuary of landscape, air, and light hidden within the skyline of Lower Manhattan.

Upon circulating through the interior of the house, it becomes apparent that through the fourteenth floor is an opening that is much larger than the opening cut through the roof. This is a second act. The courtyard previously read as negative and hollow in relation to the roof, but now it reads as a complete volume, nested within a new interior void. Views open to the thirteenth floor below, and a narrow bridge spans across the house from east to west. As the courtyard's underside is exposed, one begins to sense a weightlessness to the taut glassy volume hovering in a generously proportioned double-height space.

The second cut down through the fourteenth floor aligns neatly to a solid volume—a soft, white monolith. This solid service core for the building contains fire stairs, elevators, closets, and bathrooms. In contrast to the crisp glossiness of the courtyard, the matte surface of the core absorbs light and undulates with an articulated geometry.

While this white volume appears singular and elemental, it is actually clad in more than 600 plaster tiles, each 6 inches wide and 7 feet tall. Yet, there are no visible joints. The mass reads as a solid artifact—25 feet wide by 30 feet long and 25 feet tall—visible within a void unexpectedly spanning two floors through the historic structure.

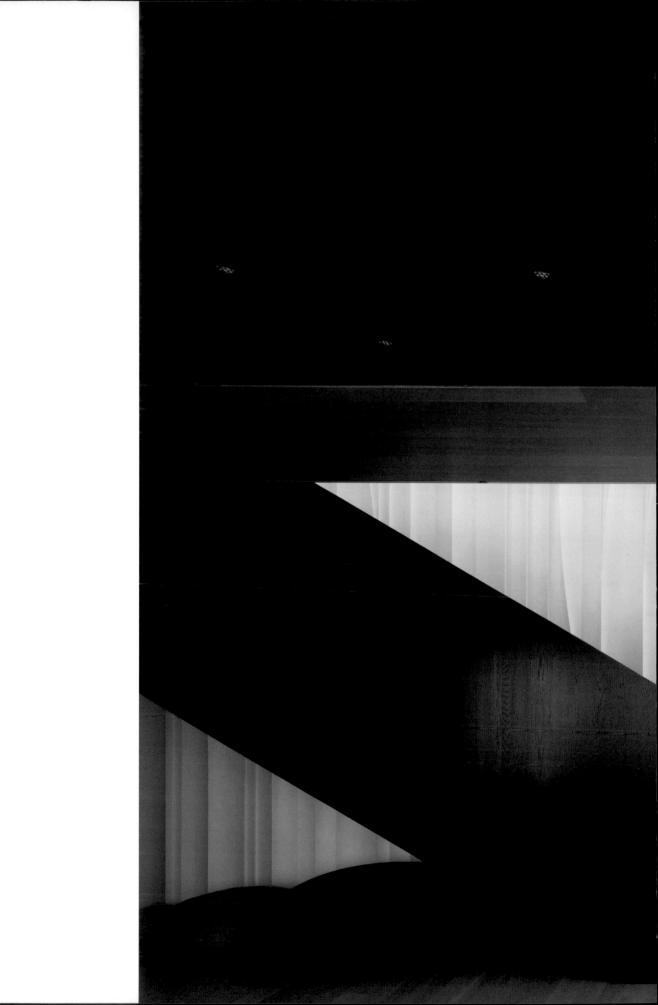

Pulled Plaster House

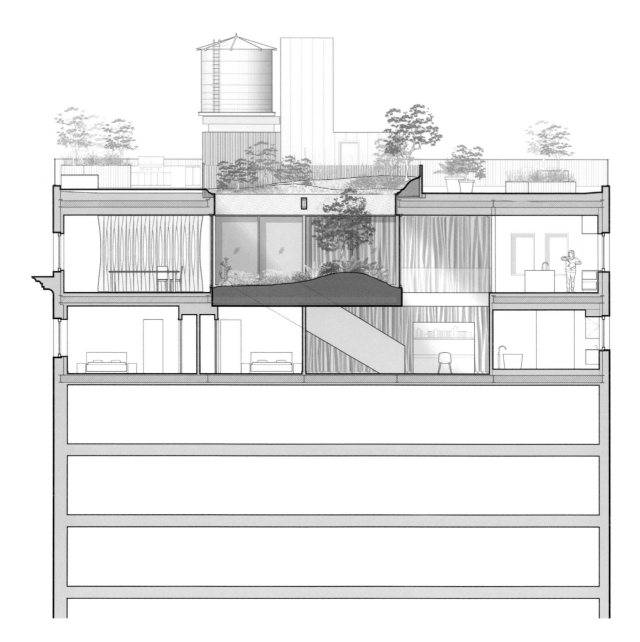

1. Breakfast Room
2. Open to below
3. Exterior courtyard
4. Dining Room
5. Living room
6. Pantry
7. Powder Room
8. Kitchen
9. Bridge
10. Primary Bathroom
11. Family room

12. Bedroom one
13. Bedroom two
14. Playroom
15. Bathroom
16. Laundry
17. Bedroom three
18. Bedroom four
19. Study
20. Closet
21. Primary bedroom

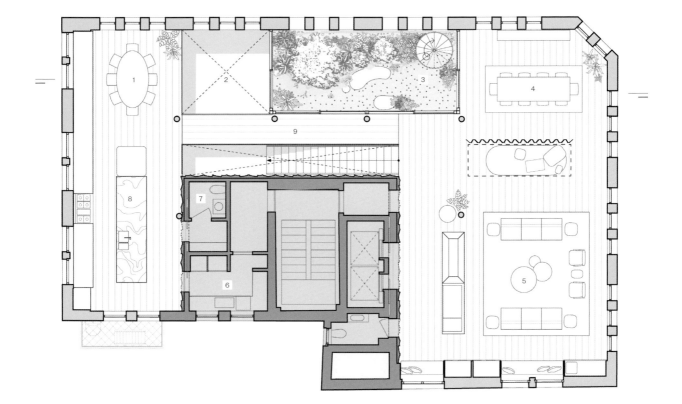

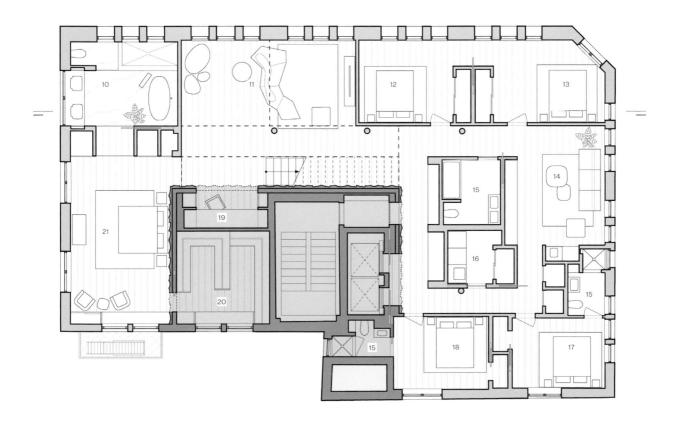

It was a happy accident that we stumbled upon the traditional technique of pulling plaster, used to make crown and base moldings for centuries. The equipment for pulling plaster consists of three basic components: the horse, which holds the knife (a two-dimensional metal profile), which is pulled along a straight rail. To pull a traditional molding is a repetitive process that takes several minutes. Liquid gypsum plaster is poured in a line down a flat work surface, then the horse and knife slide down the rail to corral the runny mixture into shape. This process is repeated multiple times as, over the course of minutes, the plaster mixture begins to hydrate and its texture changes from runny to thick to gelatinous. As the wet and goopy plaster slowly solidifies, each repeated pull of the knife compresses and trowels the surface of the molding, creating a smooth and dense finish.

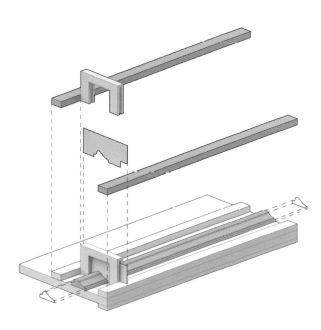

Historically, the equipment for pulling plaster has worked quite success-
fully and therefore has had little need of interrogation or improvement. The
profile of the metal knife can be cut and customized to any shape desired,
and when fixed into the horse and dragged along a straight rail, endless
profiles can be extruded.

Our intervention was simply to decouple the knife from the horse to allow the knife to move laterally throughout the length of the pull. Practically, this manifested as three unique rails to guide the motion of the knife, now sliding side to side within the horse.

One rail veered on an angle, one followed an S curve, and one was straight and parallel with the direction of the pull (as in the traditional method). This added a degree of freedom for the movement of the knife and allowed us to explore the possibility of pulling profiles beyond the straight extrusions of traditional moldings into the three-dimensional realm of lofts and sweeps.

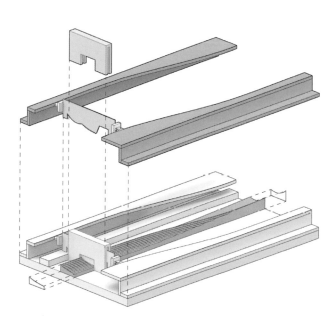

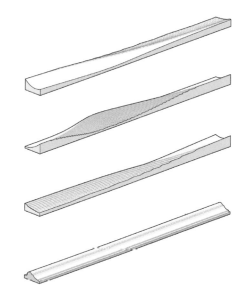

We studied and experimented with multiple knife profiles, refining the scale and shape of a singular cusp that varied from smooth to serrated. We eventually scaled the serration so that as the sawtooth neared the peak of the cusp it would decrease in depth as an elegant, soft transition to the smooth side of the tile. Conversely, as the sawtooth moved farther from the cusp it would increase in depth to accentuate shadows at the deepest moments of concavity.

The S curve was used to generate tiles that are justified to be left serrated (3A), mirrored right serrated (3B), and smooth (2A and 2B). Similarly, the straight pull generated tiles that are justified to be left or right serrated (4L, 4R) and left or right smooth (1L, 1R). The straight pulls do not have the left- or right-handedness of the S curve and therefore do not require a mirror. In the end, just two rails produced eight master pulls.

The tiles can be deployed in numerous combinations exploring aggregated geometries from straight to curved and smooth to textured. The final arrangement examines distinct moments of continuity along serrated edges and occasional discontinuities along vertical edges.

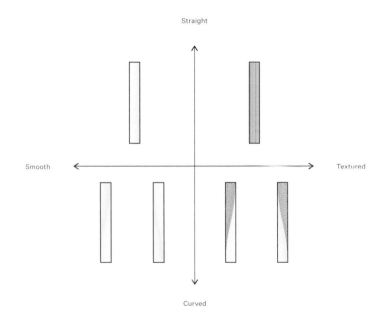

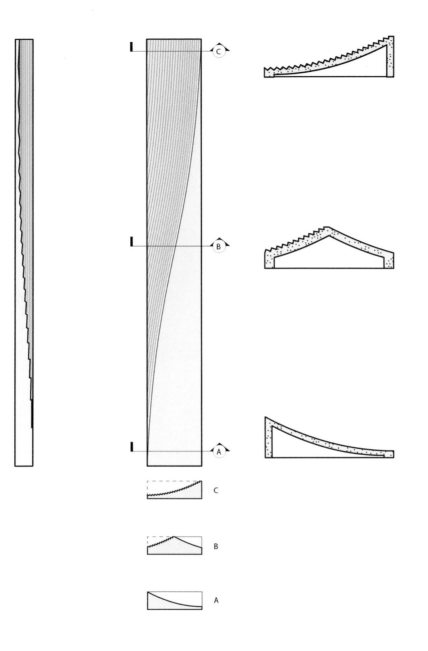

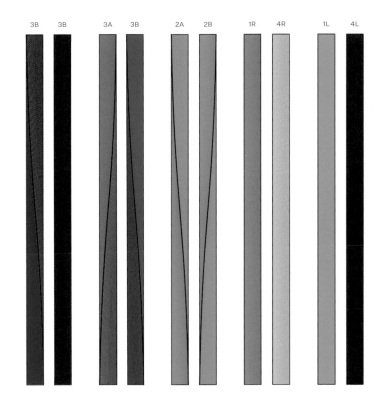

3B 3B   3A 3B   2A 2B   1R 4R   1L 4L

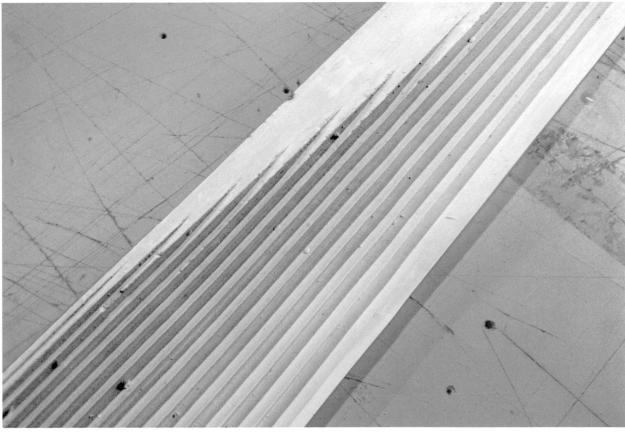

Pulled Plaster Panels

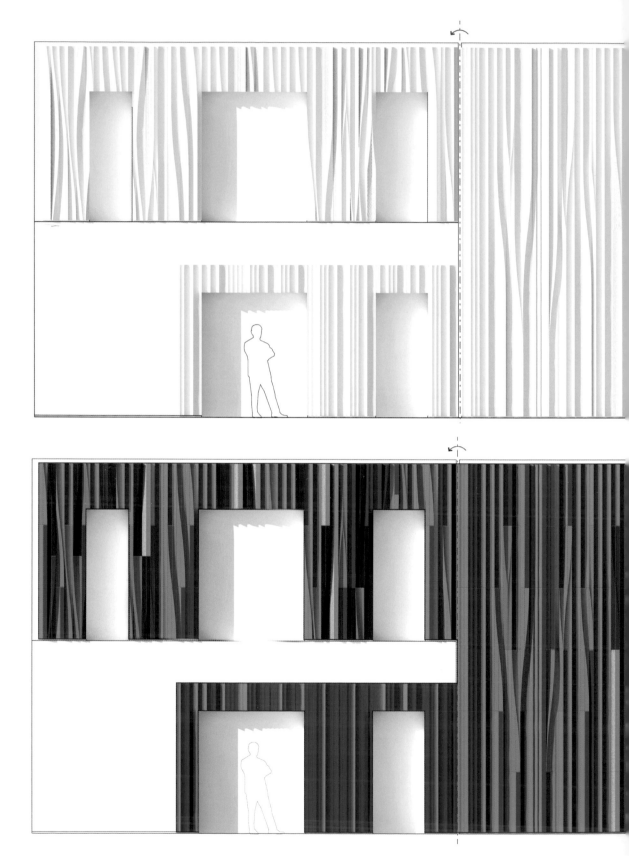

Unfolded core elevations: mapping the eight master tiles

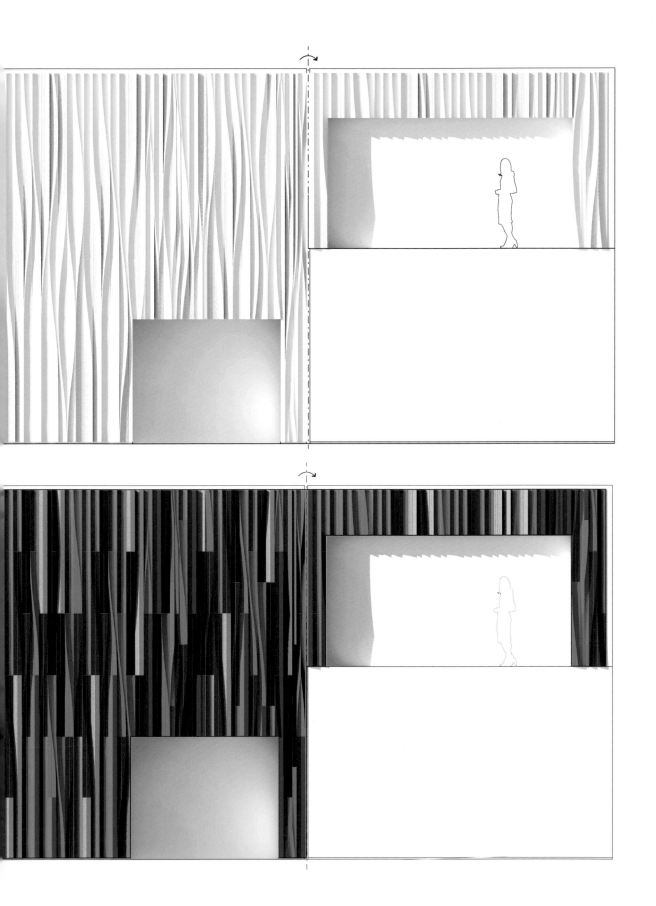

When inspecting the finished core of the Pulled Plaster House, one might erroneously assume it is perhaps an assembly of CNC-milled lumber. The depth of the undulating surface rules out a sheet material such as medium-density fiberboard (MDF). Yet, the surface continuity across the volume, the lack of any apparent joints, and the aesthetic and tactile softness signal that the volume is not clad in wood. The tectonics of the plaster panels work to subtly defamiliarize and obscure the material legibility of the core, producing an ambiguity that asks one to look closer and further engage the surface fluctuations.

Our material research often focuses on tweaking a technique for fabrication. In the case of the Pulled Plaster Tiles, it is the combination of plaster's intrinsic qualities as a material in tandem with our manipulation of the process of pulling that resulted in the novel prototype. The Pulled Plaster Tiles are simple and economic, using a fully analog, age-old methodology to produce complex and highly replicable geometries.

The versatility and seamless aesthetics of plaster that we discovered while working on the Pulled Plaster House led us to explore other possibilities for the material in a variety of forms. One such study, initially conceived as part of a proposal for the New York–based art institution The Kitchen, found success as a prototype but took a more circuitous route to finding a home in a final built project. This case study perhaps best exemplifies the nonlinear approach we often engage with when working on projects: both top down (what is specifically applicable to a given project?) and bottom up (how can a specific idea be incorporated to a given project?). Engaging a design from both directions establishes a dialogue in which the material and spatial attributes of a project work cohesively and inform one another. We are problem solving and problem making.

The initial idea for this new plaster prototype came about while working on the invited competition for the renovation and expansion of The Kitchen, currently residing in a building of several stories just off the High Line. In looking at the history of the multidisciplinary institution, we found the previous homes of The Kitchen to be compelling in ways beyond the traditional black box theater. The first locations of the budding performance space were located in the cast iron lofts of 1980s SoHo, where aspects rich in architectural character, such as ornamental column capitals and decorative moldings, ran right through the middle of dance, performance art, and soundscapes. For our proposal to update The Kitchen's Chelsea space, we proposed a traditional black box theater and gallery spaces to meet the institution's current needs, but also proposed a "white box" theater to create a *charged* performance environment with its own character.

1. Roof theater
2. Staff offices
3. Gallery
4. Black box theater
5. Lobby

We envisioned plaster panels with rippling vertical forms along the walls and sculptural overtly ornamental figures on the ceiling as the material for this white box theater. The verticality and nature of the organic geometry was both generally referential to known precedents like cathedrals, yet foreign in the specificity of its forms. The proposed construction of the panels was intended to diffuse reverberation of sound waves within the space, providing a potential performance benefit suited to the theater's use.

Although the selection committee did not award us the commission and the initial design for The Kitchen was not built, our prototyping work on the plaster concept felt promising and worth exploring further. In conjunction with Brooklyn-based plaster artisan Nathan Frey at MW Plaster we developed a prototype panel that opened up the door for future exploration. Rather than leaving the geometry of the panels open to completely willful form-making (as could be accomplished digitally and, by extension, fabricated by CNC means), we went a decidedly more analog route—both out of financial concerns as well as curiosity about the making process. Ultimately, we landed on a technique of making casting formwork from upholstery foam, hand-bent metal pencil rods, and heavy plastic sheeting that allowed some control over the general nature of the panels yet surrendered the specific aspects of curvature, voluptuousness, and surface tension over to forces beyond our control (though inherent to the materials with which we were working).

This hybrid methodology provided a framework where critical points of geometry could be controlled as necessary, variations in the physical form could be quickly iterated, and the formwork could be reused for multiple casts.

The next opportunity for deploying our plaster panels came on The Wells, a proposal for turning an existing underground concrete bunker into a wellness space featuring a series of baths: sound, salt, and smoke. The plaster panels proposed for The Wells were similar to those for The Kitchen in that mediating soundwaves in the sound bath were a primary functional objective. However, the formal nature of the panels for The Wells reflected our accumulated knowledge from prototype development, explored a more restrained geometry that thoughtfully considered some of the implications of production, and relied on tiling, mirroring, and rotating repetitive panels for graphic ornamental effect. Our client ultimately did not move forward with this project, but they did like the proposal.

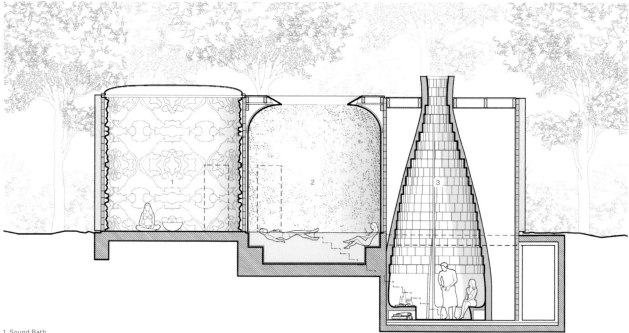

1. Sound Bath
2. Salt Bath
3. Sweat Bath

Amagansett, New York, 2019

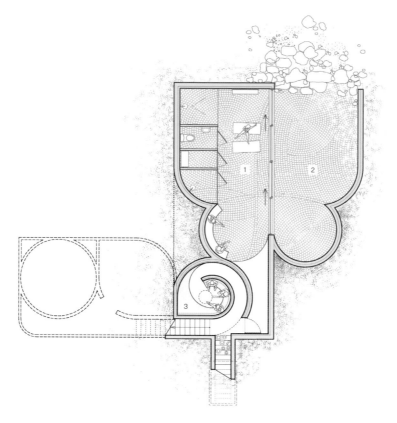

1. Meditation and Yoga Room
2. Sunken Courtyard
3. Sweat Bath
4. Sound Bath
5. Salt Bath
6. Sweat Bath

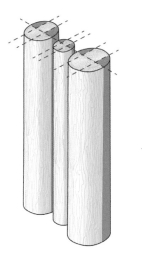 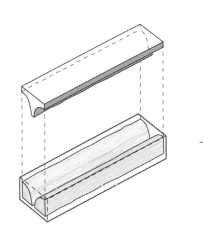 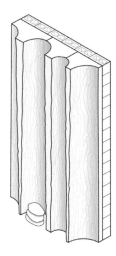

Three indigenous tree species found on site are used to create the casting molds.

The trunks are sliced and arranged in the frame to create the formwork, the negative of which is a single concrete panel.

The panels are tilted up and anchored vertically side by side, creating a facade with a textured, tapered, concave relief. The exterior can be read as a sculptural mass of petrified wood, a mausoleum, or a portal to an underworld.

Success for these cast plaster panels ultimately came in their third act, as a ceiling installation in a small New York pied-à-terre designed as a guest residence for meditation workshops. Utilizing many of the same production efficiencies explored for The Wells, the highly ornamental ceiling provides a soft, dramatically lit baffle for the apartment and unifies a simple floor plan of open kitchen, small seating area, and a burled-wood jewel box containing a bed and closets. Focused into a single studio room, the panels create the same surreal, immersive effect as explored in both The Kitchen and The Wells, but in a domestic context.

The repetition and organization of the sculptural patterns took on a purely graphic aspect reminiscent of rosettes and moldings run amok, dynamic in form but acknowledging walls and edges in a thoughtful installation. The material deployment merged the repetition of typical 1900s tin ceilings and ornamental plaster work.

The persistence of developing the cast plaster panels through multiple prototypes is a scenario that plays out often in our work. Although the role of the panels shifted from project to project, investigating the panels in a new context led to iterative revisions to the panels that continuously tailored the proposal. Each new opportunity built on the trials and errors explored in previous iterations and expanded our sense of how the panels could be used and fabricated. We were opportunistic in deploying an idea but benefited from the failed opportunities in order to ultimately develop a more interesting and achievable proposal. And we were stubborn.

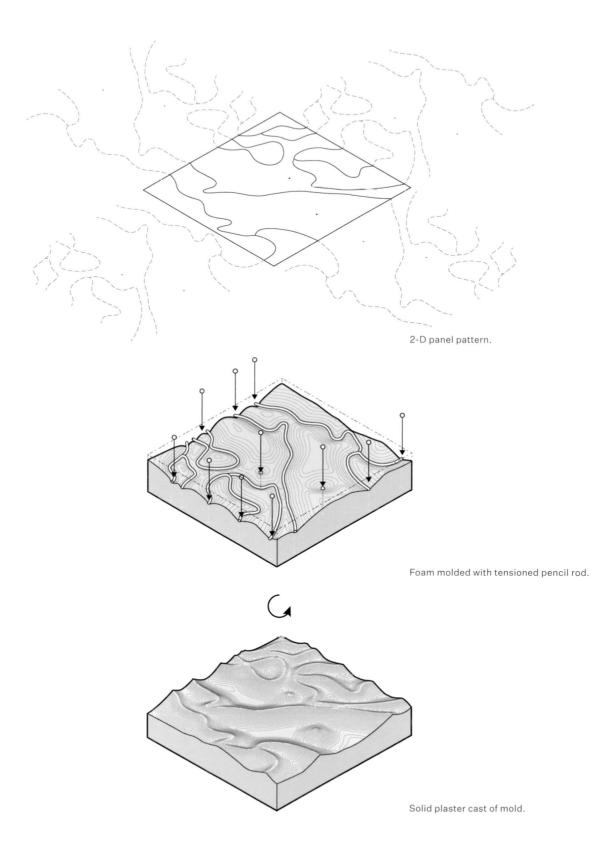

2-D panel pattern.

Foam molded with tensioned pencil rod.

Solid plaster cast of mold.

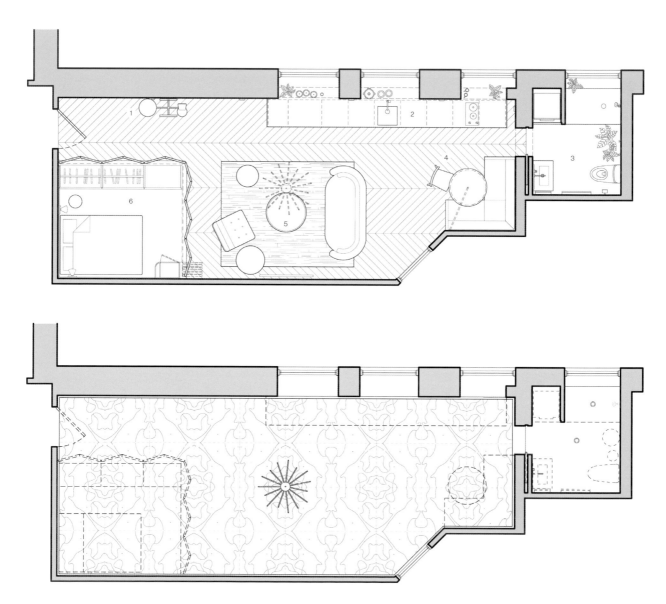

1. Foyer
2. Kitchen
3. Bathroom
4. Dining Booth
5. Living Room
6. Bedroom Volume

The tectonics of the Retreat House utilize a series of lines—in the form of trusses, battens, and palm stems—to approximate a complex curvilinear form, while at the Glitch House pixels aggregate to define a building mass with much simpler geometry. The Rock House returns to fluid forms but finds spatiality and materiality through a language of carvings—stereotomic rather than tectonic.

The Rock House is hidden from the adjacent program of the Retreat House. Users come upon the beachside structure through a small path in the jungle and encounter a series of cryptic landforms cracked apart by shard-like apertures. From a distance, the house is broadly suggestive of a singular monolithic mass beginning to wear away into discrete ruinous rocks. A closer reading, however, reveals a potential inverse: six carefully controlled forms, unified through acts of symmetry, alignment, tangency, and repetition. A continuous cropping envelope and brutalist concrete finish further this ambiguity; the structure is both a bunker and a collection of unearthed stones.

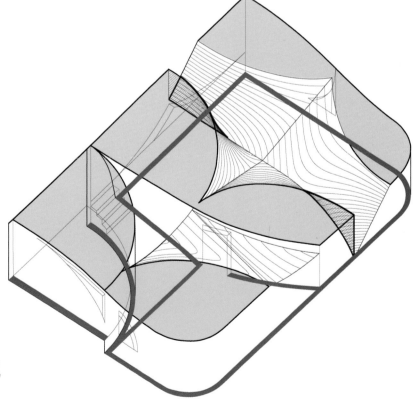

Worm's eye view: the interior geometry of the roof follows the spatial constraints of the hammam, changing room, steam and plunge room while also allowing these programs to share a unifying volume.

The program for the Rock House includes a primary open chamber with a changing and arrival area, a marble hammam, a steam room, and a cold plunge pool. Off the main area is a small powder room and a cedar sauna. Outside, there is an open-air massage room accessed from the beach. The room is bounded by overlapping arching planes that allow cross ventilation to flow east to west.

The building is small and meant for no more than four guests at a time. To enter the structure, a guest descends five steps through a crescent-shaped gap on the north elevation. Upon arriving in the main chamber, the form of the exterior is revealed to be closely tied to the performative needs of the four programs. In the chamber, four adjacent quadrants come together; they are continuous yet spatially distinct. The hammam has a twelve foot ceiling at its highest edge, facing out to panoramic views of the ocean and horizon. The roof above the steam room bows down to seven feet to contain the wet heat and facilitate the required thermodynamics. The cold plunge pool is scaled for individual use and the changing room is illuminated by a single round skylight. The formal spectacle of the roof works dynamically to subtly subdivide a small chamber into intimate spaces without reducing the experience to a series of separate and sealed spaces.

1. Hammam
2. Changing
3. Entry
4. Massage
5. Sauna
6. Powder Room
7. Plunge
8. Steam

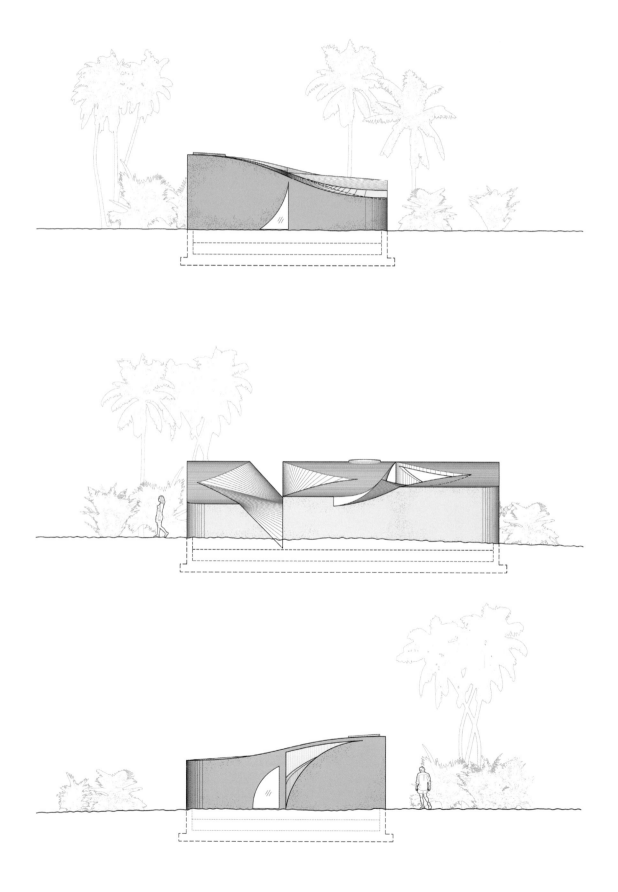

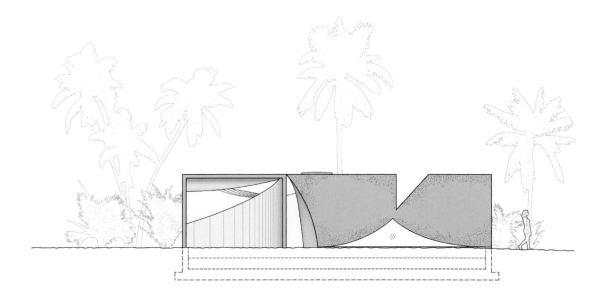

The material investigation for the Rock House is deeply intertwined with the spatial narrative of the overall project. Entitled Twice-Baked Concrete, the material emerges from a process of deliberately chipping site-cast structural concrete to reveal pockets of color and texture.

The concrete's color is the result of first casting sacrificial concrete slabs toned with a vibrant teal integral colorant, then breaking these slabs into small pieces to be reused as a coarse aggregate. This highly colored, synthesized coarse aggregate was added to a concrete mix with white cement, white fine aggregate, and a white admix designed to yield a pristine off-the-form surface texture and homogeneous color. The technique proved effective and economical in comparison to terrazzo-like alternative aggregates such as quartz, recycled glass, marble, or other natural stones.

The chipping involves a carefully directed and deliberate hand process intended to evoke the temporal effects of erosion. Once the taut white skin of the site-cast concrete begins to deteriorate, the pores of coloration emerge and read as an aging patina or stubborn moss. Yet, this type of artificial decay is incongruent with the intentionality of the building's form, the crispness of its corners, and its sharply excised apertures. The contradiction of the building's volumetric precision relative to its rugged surface materiality generates an ambiguity that is more than skin deep, asking visitors to look more closely.

The Twice-Baked Concrete is consciously graphic and responsive to the form of the Rock House, as the top edges and corners feature the most heavily distressed material, gradually softening down to clean white concrete. Our research into this material process, as with the encaustic cement tiles used at the Glitch House, was conducted within an architectural milieu interested in the relationship and potential interferences of graphics relative to legibility of form. While developing the Rock House, this friction was initially studied through a series of speculative 3-D prints as part of the *New Practices New York 2016* exhibition at the Center for Architecture.

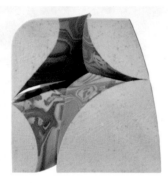

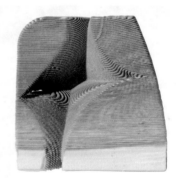

Prior to resolving the precise procedures for Twice-Baked Concrete, we hoped to push the materiality of "malformed" concrete for the Rock House even further. We were particularly interested in "honeycombing," which occurs when wet concrete is insufficiently vibrated, allowing air pockets to remain in the formwork and typically exposing areas of coarse aggregate. An entirely different (though similarly named and similarly aesthetic) honeycombing also occurs naturally along stone surfaces that are eroded near the sea due to forces such as marine abrasion and wind. In developing Twice-Baked Concrete, we had hoped to allow a similar degradation of materiality as an aesthetic and even formal organizer. However, it became impossible, as the intensity of the desired visual effect was inversely proportional to the concrete's durability and structural strength.

Just as the Rock House can be read as a six-pack of forms that come together to shape a whole, the Elephant Table is conceived as a family of six similar stones. Related in form and materiality, the six pieces are individual elements gathered to compose an imperfect whole. Conversely, the table is a singular form dissolving into six independent shapes with delicate fault lines and subtle idiosyncrasies. Each of the stones has a mesa quartzite top and a cream limestone base that allow the individual pieces to be visually delicate yet balanced and stable.

The two largest stones are bound together and structurally anchor the four smaller stones. The family assumes new figures as the stones are reorganized, but the arrangement is only truly settled when all six pieces align and the graining of the mesa quartzite flows from piece to piece. In fact, the origination of all six stones from a single quartzite slab is the fingerprint that unlocks the puzzle of putting the table back together. Particular attention was given to defining the boundary geometries for each piece. As adjacent stones meet, their soft, rolled edges rationalize into orthogonal corners, and the stone's grain bridges seamlessly. Moving away from shared faces of contact, the edges gain independence and soften to reveal the grain as the volumetric materiality knitted through the thickness of each stone.

It is within the realm of craft—from prototyping small material samples to fabricating at the scale of building finishes—that the work of my company, Paola Lenti, and that of Young Projects significantly overlap. We share a deep fascination in the exploration of materials as an expression of the process of making, which we have collaboratively explored in the Cluster and Tilt tile series that are currently in production. Through extensive experimentation with characteristics inherent in various materials, we search for ways to create something new, something of material substance that viscerally communicates unexpected forms, colors, textures, and articulated surfaces. Additionally, we share a dedication to collaborating with master craftspeople whose traditions have been passed to them from previous generations, the artisans whose skilled hands and techniques transform our inspirations into physicalness.

Paola Lenti and Young Projects are also aligned in the foundational tenets of ecological responsibility and the roles that our companies can play in sustainable prototyping and production. Responding to climate change demands a substantive reconsideration of not only the way we design but also how we manufacture. We continue to pursue production methods to reduce our impact upon the environment and on human and animal life by embracing concepts that support biodiversity within manufacturing. We have made strides in reducing waste and increasing the recyclability at the end of a product's useful life. At Paola Lenti, our

continuous research has allowed us to enhance the sustainability of signature outdoor yarns, cords, braids, and fabrics. We have introduced new materials, like the Twiggy yarn and Diade textile, which are fully recyclable and have improved resistance and durability promoting their longevity. In addition to designing high-tech materials, the company has turned its attention to vegetable fibers, with a preference for herbaceous and shrubby plants with seasonal growth such as linen, hemp, and bamboo, obtained thanks to the careful control of the supply chain and to traditional cultivation techniques. At the same time, our design process aims to reduce the components of each product to facilitate disposal at the end of its life.

As a result of this, the prototypes we have designed with Young Projects have examined fabrication and manufacturing techniques as a central focus for sustainability. Young Projects' Pulled Plaster House is a unique architectural example in which the design focused extensively on creating a new type of plaster tile not through design, but rather through reconsidering manufacturing. The geometry and texture of the tiles is the result of only slightly changing a traditional technique with a plaster artisan, yet the resulting tiles are distinctly contemporary. In forming or casting the pulled plaster tiles there is significantly less waste than if the material was milled with wood. At Paola Lenti, we found this research refreshing, as the concept for the prototype originates from examining the process of making; rather than forcing a visual aesthetic, the pulled plaster tiles are an act of revealing.

The tiles for the Pulled Plaster House inspired a collaboration entitled Tilt in which a ceramic tile is the result of inserting kneaded clay in a unique mold; we then emboss the moist clay with a fabric texture, and finally fire the tile with colored glaze. Despite following a set sequence of design rules, each tile is slightly different. The organic properties of the clay, the pigmentation in the colored glaze, and the loose patterning of the textile resist replication even though we are working with a highly defined process. We are continuing to develop Tilt with the intent to reduce the production stages to a single step.

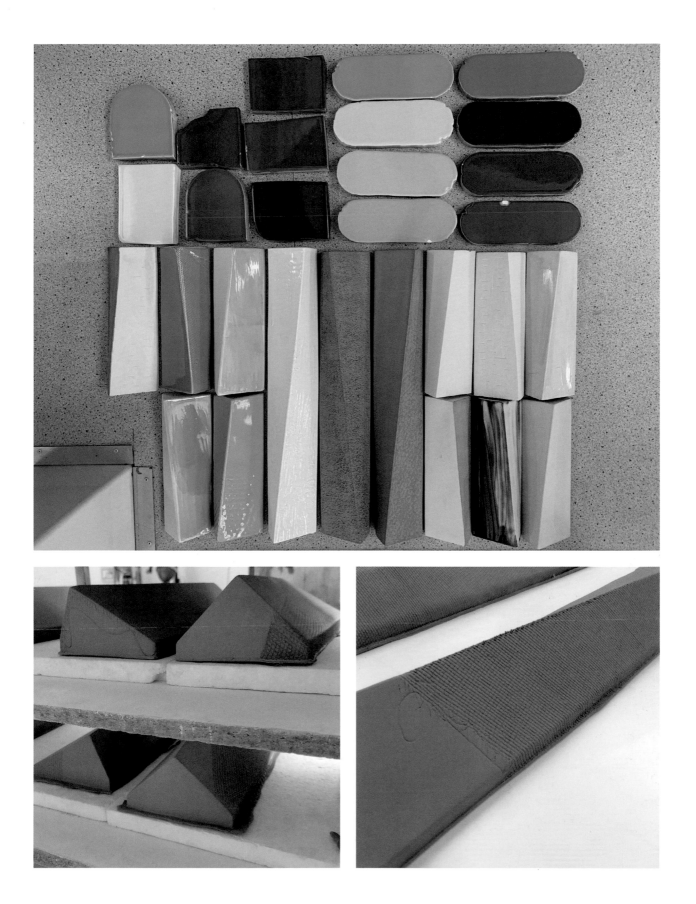

The second tile we created together is entitled Cluster. The design for this tile began as an extension of the concrete and aggregate experiments Young Projects developed for the Rock House. In Cluster, various colors of cement are cast with recycled stone and marble splinters into a soft, rounded form. The top of the tile is then sliced to expose the cluster of the contrasting aggregates.

As with many of the products we have developed at Paola Lenti, the Cluster tile utilizes efficiency of machine production in tandem with hand-made interventions. It is a hybrid process, and a special beauty emerges between qualities of machine fabrication, manual processes, and natural organic formation. This is a characteristic feature of our entire production. Many of our textile pieces are woven by hand with industrially manufactured cords and braids. They are then shaped manually into modules, which are assembled and finished by hand by skilled artisans.

In all of our work, we seek to bridge the gap between architecture and decor. Inspired by many great architects, who designed pieces and finishes specifically for each house or building, we want to create a series of products that establish a seamless transition between the architectural elements, the decorative finishes, and the furniture and objects that are living within a space. Prior to meeting Bryan and working with Young Projects, we had already begun this ambition, and it is with deep admiration for Young Projects' architecture, material research, and prototypes that we continue our synergetic partnership.

Cluster: Building on the Twice-Baked Concrete experiments developed for the Rock House, our first design collaboration with Paola Lenti examined similar relationships of geometry, texture, and color at the scale of an architectural product. In the Cluster tiles, we used the same ingredients—homogenous smooth cement and colored coarse aggregate—but confined their interaction to a single tile. The aggregate was revealed through slicing rather than chipping and sandblasting. We experimented with multiple color combinations in our mockups, testing different cement colors for the tile base against colored marble chips within, tweaking the level of contrast between cement and aggregate. The final two colorways selected for the collection are a teal cement base with white aggregate and a soft white cement base with black aggregate.

For the Cluster collection, we decided on two inclinations for each of the two colorways. The result is a series of 3-D square tiles with graphically contrasting circles and semicircles. When assembled and deployed at an architectural scale, the repetition and rotation of the two tile types together can create a playful irregularity and dynamic movement across the tiled surface, while each individual tile appears to contain floating abstracted elements, frozen in a moment of suspension.

Tilt: The studies for Tilt began by examining ways of manually manipulating clay in the earliest stages of the design process: as it is extruded for manual ceramic work. We looked specifically at the rotation of a rectangular extrusion and how to capture the resultant curved edges in our

Bryan Young

rectangular tiles. We studied different degrees of rotation and how to cut and slice the clay at different scales to achieve individual tiles.

Once the final tile forms had been selected (one tile and its inverse), we created molds for the base geometries. At this stage, the tiles were geometrically identical, aside from the interesting and inevitable minor irregularities that arise from manual handling of the clay and the firing process. Before firing, we wanted to introduce a more intentional manual intervention, enriching the tactile quality and individuality of each tile. In some tiles the texture adheres to the geometric logic of the tile, having one smooth surface and the other textured. Other tiles received texture throughout, or had texture applied at an angle, misaligned with the sharp formal edges of the tiles.

The tiles in the Tilt collection capture a small portion of a larger rotated geometry, resulting in soft, subtly curving edges. We are expanding on the Tilt collection, developing a new series of tiles that capture tighter twists and rotations. These tiles are slices through a geometry that has undergone a more dramatic rotation, creating round, swooping edges in each tile. When assembled into a larger overall tiled surface, the ridges align vertically to evoke a continuous, thick, coiled cord, giving an alluring woven textile quality.

Bryan Young

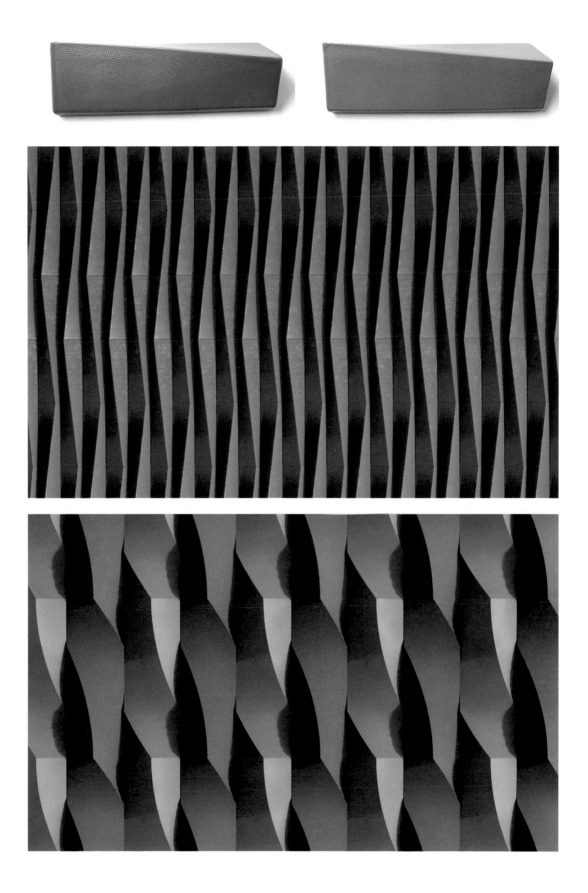

Six Square House

Triaxially symmetrical squares, large and small
equilateral triangles, and isosceles triangles

The design for the Six Square House in Bridgehampton, New York, originates from a continuous 2-D tessellation of squares, large and small equilateral triangles, and isosceles triangles. As the base plan for the house, it creates a tight, clustering pattern that is triaxially symmetric. While this 2-D composition follows a strict internal geometry, the house reveals a complex and nuanced spatial proposition and an unexpectedly sensitive connection with the adjacent landscape. This is the beginning of an intriguing tension between the apparent indifference of the pattern's abstract footprint and the physical idiosyncrasies of site, program, and structure.

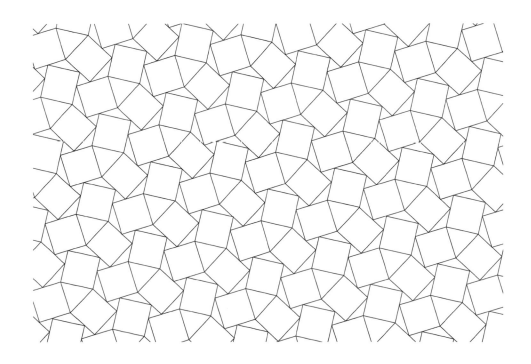

Six Square House

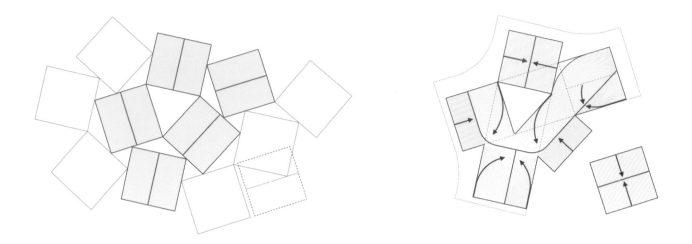

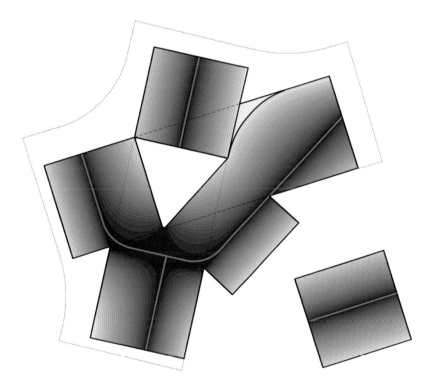

To create a continuous eave line, soft arcs are
introduced along the facades which in turn leads
to gentle ruled surfaces at the roof/ceiling.

Beginning with a 2-D diagram that is neutral relative to the site and following with an internally motivated geometric study, may seem to be a strange way to design a house as it puts the cart before the horse. However, it is a highly productive nonlinear process in which ideas of space and structure are examined in tandem with the parameters of context: program, use, landscape, and, most importantly, the client's goals. In fact, many of the projects presented in this book are the result of the manner in which a nonlinear design process merges multiple design parameters into highly complex material and spatial propositions.

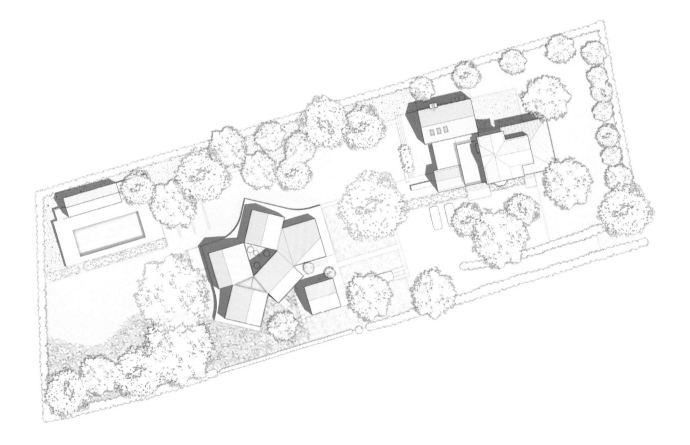

At the Six Square House, the 2-D diagram implies vertical extrusion to define a set of rooms. The resolution of the extrusion undermines the legibility of its own origin to create a spatially charged figure resulting from not only the transformation of the gabled typology but also the way in which seemingly discrete rooms are tied together at points of intersection. This translation from a 2-D origin to 3-D resolution sets off a series of oscillating readings that fuel the spatial ambiguity prevalent in the final project. The most explicit ambiguity is the dialectic reading of the autonomous volumes legible on the exterior contrasted with the continuously flowing spaces of the interior. This tension manifests through a highly specific choreography of geometric alignments, offsets, arcs, and projections.

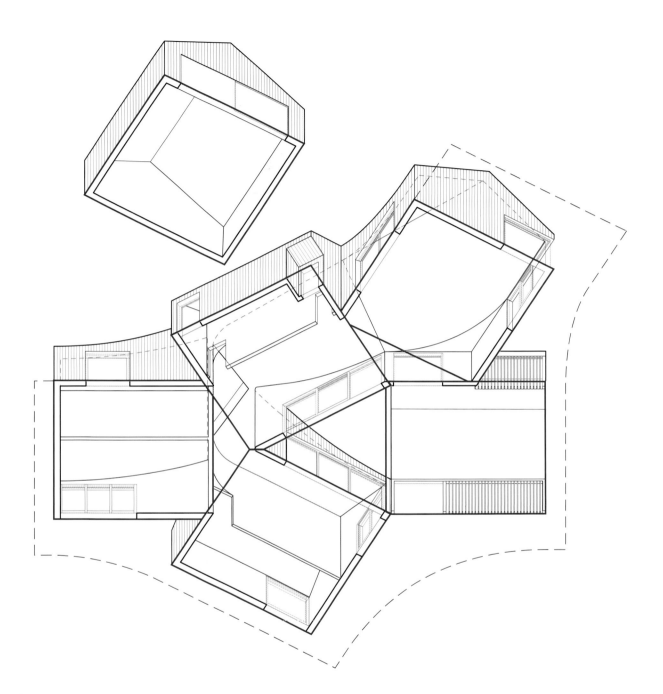

Worm's eye view showing the six discrete
squares along with the sinuous ceiling plane
and flowing geometry

Six Square House

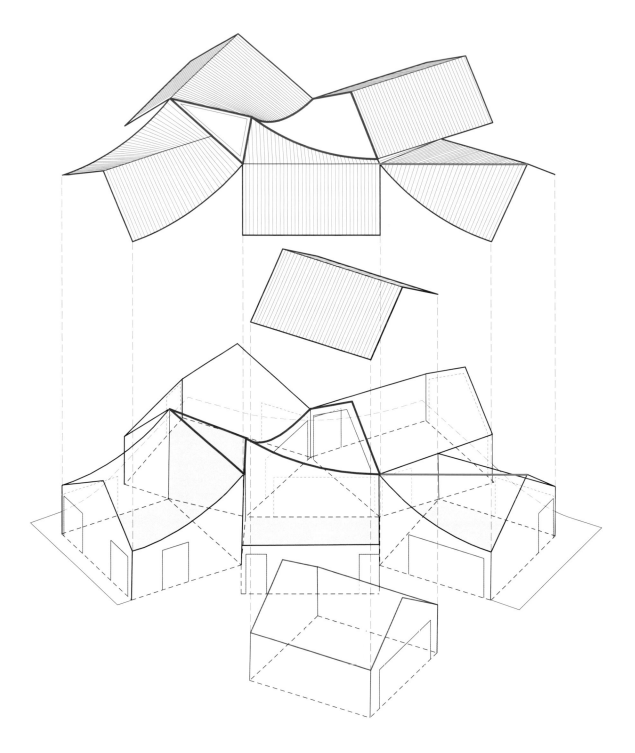

The roof geometry follows a ruled surface that
negotiates a gabled end with a horizontal plane
following a ridge transposed from one square
to the next.

Each square of the house is programmed to consider adjacency, degree of privacy, and relationships to the other structures.

(1) Starting at the top, an open-air porch space serves as an outdoor lounge and the central dining pavilion for the entire property.

(2) The living room is an expansive space with southern glazing and a corner window looking toward a historic farmhouse to the northeast. This view is reinforced by a diagonal roof ridge projecting from the high point of the kitchen volume (3) in the adjoining square to the southwest.

(4) The next square contains the primary bedroom suite with a corner window looking toward a private garden and old-growth purple beech tree.

(5) A guest bedroom and den space look upon the "leftover" triangular court anchoring the cluster.

(6) The last square has fallen off the pattern and shares a moment of orthogonal alignment with the living room square to the north. This compositional decision creates a scene of arrival in which two symmetrical gable structures comprise a flat facade. In this way a stage set attempts to pose as if it had accumulated accessory barn structures.

(7) However, enough geometry is already revealed at the entry court to know something has gone awry.

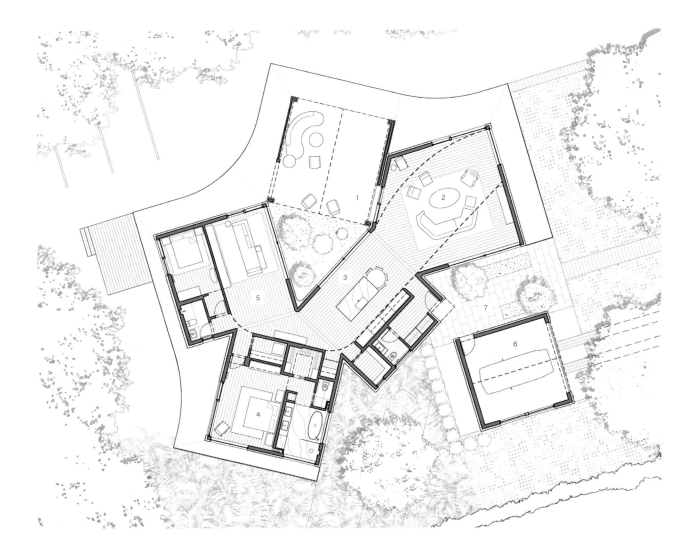

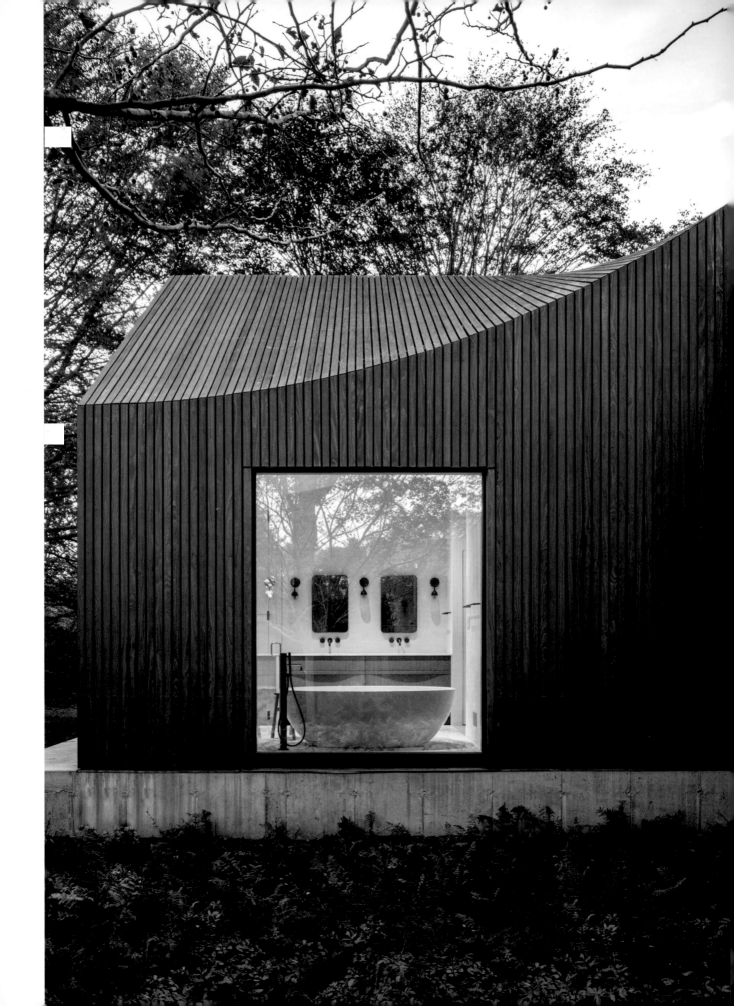

The design for the Six Square House begins with an internal geometric logic and typological reference in the form of a gabled barn; through multiple transformations, a dynamic figure emerges with a radical organization for a house. In parallel, an alternate presentation could easily develop as follows: there are a series of critical site relationships to the immediate landscape, existing historic farmhouse, pool house, and path of the sun that organize and orient six gabled volumes at the center of the property. In this narrative, it is relevant but secondary that the plan contains squares, equilateral triangles, and isosceles triangles. The six squares—with deliberately oriented gabled frames and curated apertures—act as a series of lenses for looking out. The rooms are organized sequentially to rationalize circulation and provide access to the exterior environments and gardens. They create shared open spaces toward the front (north and east) and tuck away the private spaces toward the back (south and west). Critical existing trees, most importantly the purple beech tree to the west and psychedelic oak to the east, bind the siting of the six squares as well as arrange the corner windows.

There are numerous existing site conditions: mature trees, stormwater runoff and solar shading, as well as relationships of program and circulation that inform the layout and massing. Additionally, a second set of curated landscape and hardscape design moves further root the house in its context. Specimen trees focus views, clusters of trees create intimacy, and the gabled volumes of the Six Square House strike up a respectful dialogue with the historic gabled farmhouse. The Six Square House is both an object to be viewed in the round and a device that frames an experience with a specific context—existing and constructed—and program.

The six volumes of the house reveal the varying degrees to which the neutral pattern of the 2-D plan and gabled typology have been transformed. Upon arrival, one understands the aligned facades of symmetrical gabled cubes (the garage and living room, separated by the entry court) as the departing reference point. Rotating counterclockwise around the house, the next volume is the open-air patio. While also symmetrical when viewed head on, the roof ridge of the patio volume plays an important role in framing the central equilateral central courtyard. The edge of the patio volume comprises one of the three sides of the equilateral court, but the fact that it is a gable end means that this one "straight" side becomes two peaked segments when translated into three dimensions: the three-sided figure seen in plan becomes a four-sided figure in space. This extra hitch in the patio volume overlays the arcing eave lines of the living room and kitchen volumes beyond as they curve up to align with the high point of the ridge. The equilateral triangle extracted from the tessellated plan manifests as a complex, volumetric boundary tracing connecting edges of the roof line.

Geometric deviations grow in complexity as one continues with the next volume to the west (revolving counterclockwise around the cluster.) This volume has an asymmetrical ridgeline, separating one ruled roof surface from another, which is a flat, sloped shed roof. Continuing to rotate around the house, the next volume, which contains the primary bedroom suite, again has an asymmetrical ridgeline but with two ruled roof surfaces of different widths. One curving surface gracefully lifts above the bedroom while the other rises above the bathroom. At this point, the typology of the gabled roof has morphed to become a series of hybrids: equally gabled, shed, salt box, and flat roof.

Like the Rock House and the related Elephant Table, the Six Square House can be considered a six-pack, playing on an ambiguity of part to whole. All three projects have discrete pieces that precariously touch, suggesting the potential (but incomplete) resolution of a singular entity. The oscillation between part and whole at the Six Square House, unlike at the Rock House and in the Elephant Table, is an even more intense enigma, as one must reconcile the exterior tectonics—straight pieces of lumber approximating complex geometries—with the immaterial abstraction of the interiors—smooth, soft masses continuously flowing around and through the various volumes.

Even more confounding is the realization that the interior and exterior are almost entirely a one-to-one pairing, the simplest and most direct resolution of gypsum wallboard and wood siding applied over plain dimensional lumber. There is no trickery, fluff, or sleight of hand in the construction, and yet the two readings are extraordinarily difficult to reconcile.

The two narratives of the Six Square House happen in tandem. This is indicative of perhaps the most critical oscillation in this book, an approach that embraces top-down and bottom-up decisions as parallels to create charged architectural environments. In earlier projects, this oscillation is understood more clearly through top-down decisions of spatiality and form negotiating with bottom-up conceptions of materiality and making. From that vantage point, the Six Square House is an outlier in that its dual narratives do not require any specific material inquiry but subsist solely on tectonic resolutions.

The process for designing the Six Square House bears similarity to Young Projects' founding principal Bryan Young's Harvard Graduate School of Design (GSD) master's thesis project on Donkey Kong and Pac-Man ("UpUpDownDownLeftRightLeft," 2003, with advisor Hashim Sarkis). In that study, actual and fictional glitches in the 2-D game environment were utilized to tease out and construct speculative resolved 3-D spaces that more faithfully fostered the actions, movements, and play seen in the game. Using Donkey Kong as an example, allowing the character Mario to navigate up through the terracing section and dodge fiery barrels would require a series of tangential offsets and inflected curves in and out of the depth of the section shown flatly on screen, shaping the exterior envelope into a series of ribbons with key moments of vertical continuity. Sinuous rather than ruled, the geometry of the Donkey Kong facade is similar to the roof of the Six Square House: offsets, projections of ridges, and internal voids are necessary to establish their critical linkages and continuities.

In the case of Pac-Man, the 3-D speculation is the result of considering the single 2-D diagram of the game board in tandem with the spatial parameters suggested by the movement and accidental but fortuitous glitches within the iconic game environment. Three overlayed elliptical mazes wrap and intersect at a "tunnel," thus providing spatial continuity across the 2-D screen and reconciling other 3-D conflicts. This establishes a set of rules from which the diagram can be mis-extruded and spatially transformed, and the speculative environment reverse engineered.

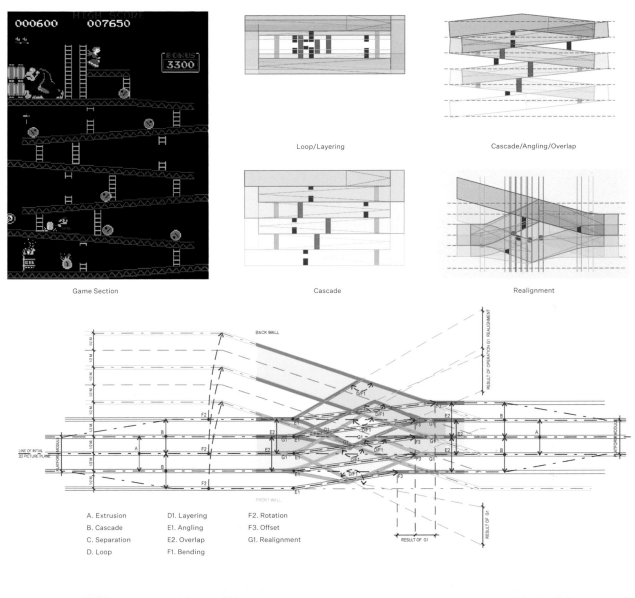

Game Section

Loop/Layering

Cascade/Angling/Overlap

Cascade

Realignment

BACK WALL

FRONT WALL

A. Extrusion
B. Cascade
C. Separation
D. Loop
D1. Layering
E1. Angling
E2. Overlap
F1. Bending
F2. Rotation
F3. Offset
G1. Realignment

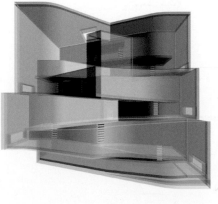

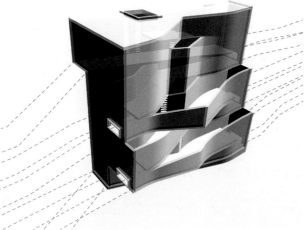

The tunnel is resolved by wrapping the 2-D diagram into a cylinder. In the game, monsters pass through each other and, due to a glitch, Pac-Man might rarely pass through a monster. While inconsistent with the more apparent rules of the game design, these conditions can be reconciled through stratification—three mazes that are offset directly on top of one other. The final transformation is to provide a reasonable intersection between the three mazes, which results in pinching the cylinder into an ellipse and realigning overlapping tunnels in plan. This reasonably allows Pac-Man or the monsters to shift between stratified layers upon entering and exiting the tunnel.

In the game environments of Pac-Man and Donkey Kong, as well as in the Six Square House (and at moments in the Retreat House, the Guest House, and the Rock House), there is heightened criticality to the conventions of a 2-D projection. The two-dimensional cut becomes the catalyst for orchestrating spatial transformation. Spatial complexity is built up from orthographic floor plans, reflected ceiling plans, section cuts, and elevations rather than the reverse model of production, in which 2-D cuts are the resultant clip of a 3-D digital model.

Working with a 2-D cut, you discover and develop spatial relationships through a speculative depth that is understood most explicitly in the abstract flattened space of a 2-D plane. Opportunities for alignments or tangents might already be lost in a 3-D model, whereas isolating the 2-D plane allows for formal resolutions that are bounded back to specific orthographic analysis. Formal choreography is conducted at arm's length, like a puppeteer and the strings to a marionette. The Six Square House falls into this narrative most clearly, as the roof geometry is constructed from the 2-D plan diagram of tessellated squares along with the 2-D elevations in which the roof eve line curves to create geometric continuity.

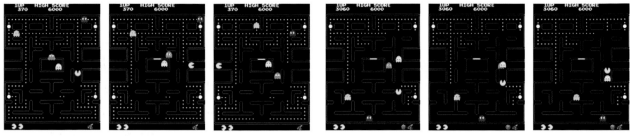

Tunnel

Layers

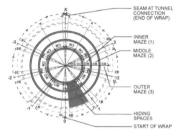

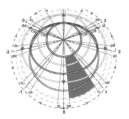

Plan diagram: cylinder scheme

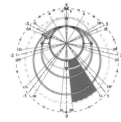

Reposition inner and middle mazes
to intersect at tunnel connection
(x)

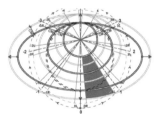

Offset inner maze
by CM module

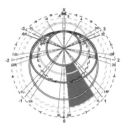

Re-scale middle maze to clear
inner CM module at line 3L/-3R

Offset module maze by
CM module

Re-scale outer maze to clear
middle CM module at line 3L/-3R

Offset outer maze
by CM module

Plan diagram: oval scheme

The origins of the Six Square House can also be found within the design of a yet-to-be-realized chandelier for the Pulled Plaster House. The chandelier utilizes a repetitive folding pattern rotated to three orientations to create a rigid waffle structure that can take on multiple global forms. The three orientations can then be cut with a laser or water jet as flat planes and flat packed for simple shipping and assembly. The three orientations of the folding pattern, when examined in plan, consist of squares, large equilateral triangles, small equilateral triangles, and isosceles triangles—the same 2-D tessellation used for the plan of the Six Square House.

In the chandelier, the geometric manipulations of the waffle pattern are ultimately cropped to define a generic and infinitely interchangeable volumetric figure at its perimeter. In the Six Square House, the unit adopts the generic (a gabled volume) only to produce a resultant open-ended figure and begin to generate its own new spatial geometries.

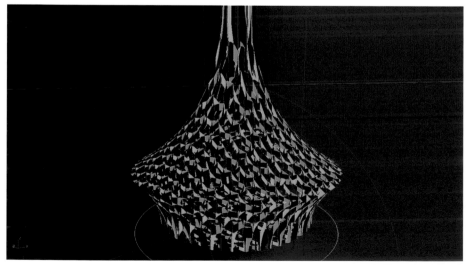
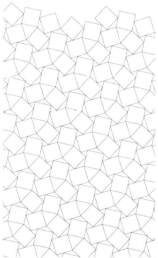

Young Projects, Six Square House, Bridgehampton, New York, 2020.

Bryan Young   Sean and Jeannette, I wanted to have this conversation with you to discuss two of your houses relative to considerations of typology and Young Projects' design for the Six Square House. Sean's Concord House and Jeannette's House on a Slope both engage the typology of a gabled house in a radical way. With the Concord House there are very interesting and unexpected geometries, and with House on a Slope there is a unique and provocative disbursement of program within a seemingly more consistent gabled volume or envelope.

In the Six Square House, we were interested in creating an ambiguity of typology through gradual transformations of the gabled profile and through an unconventional organization in plan. As a result of this approach, the Six Square House has elements that can be understood as disparate from the exterior yet at the same time continuous on the interior. Hierarchically the house is both internally organized through its own abstract compositional logics but, at the same time, thoroughly engaged in the way it addresses the external context of program and site conditions. Working back and forth between these parameters generates a productive tension.

Karamuk Kuo Architects, House on a Slope, Zollikon, Switzerland, 2020.

Jeannette Kuo   Yes, that tension between internal and external parameters can be found in all three projects, but perhaps in different ways. For the House on a Slope, we were operating in the Swiss suburbs where the majority of people are still building single-family homes. So, there are five compact, affordable units in the envelope, which is normally zoned for a single house. And the house was a commentary on how much space we really need to have or how we can interpret spatial generosity.

We wanted as much diversity as possible within these five units. Every apartment has its own characteristics, and while all units are organized with common areas, they have different configurations. Every inch counts—we were compacting everything into the maximum buildable envelope.

The site is in a very affluent neighborhood. And so the disguising of this building is an important factor. You can't tell where one unit ends and where another begins. The sizing and the juggling of the windows further make it seem like one single building.

It seems that both in Sean's Concord House and this project, we're trying to disguise density within one little thing that holds a uniform image, whereas in the Six Square House, it's about the breaking down of that single house into smaller elements so that you never see it all in one go.

Studio Sean Canty, Concord House, Concord, Massachusetts, 2019.

Sean Canty   The Concord House was also a project in trying to conceal density in a single-family neighborhood, while at the same time speculating on how models of either a co-ownership or attached accessory dwelling units (ADUs) might provide additional income for the main client. The lot is on a corner bend of a cul-de-sac with other single-family homes. In trying to maximize the allowable footprint, the house bends and contorts. The house has three units, and it was important to have a common space that all the units could share. And so the introduction of a circular rotunda became an interior commons for all three residents, but they have their own entries into the units. One is a two-story unit, a single-family home with an internal staircase. The other two units are stacked one-story flats. We worked on a few iterations of this. The flat on the upper level is smaller than that below, so there are three scales of units in one building.

In the Concord House, we tried to keep the public-facing side mostly abstract and very compositional, which conceals the number of units that are in here and concentrates more on the openings on the back.

In the center commons, the lower level is flexible space, a living room for all of the units, but at the top is a study in the conical turret. A big plane of glass brings indirect light into the interior of the dome.

Bryan Young   All three of us went to the Harvard GSD, which means we all probably had Michael Hays for theory and read Rafael Moneo's "On Typology." One statement that has always resonated with me is Moneo's assessment that type is "the frame within which change operates."

I think that all three houses are typological statements, but they are, to varying degrees, as Jeannette said, also a disguise that can be considered the frame. I'm interested in talking about this idea of disguise and how the architecture in each case reveals and deviates from its typological disguise.

House on a Slope has an iconic gabled end facade, but its roof is more like a shed, because of its slope with the topography. From a performative perspective of shedding rain, the building doesn't require the gables laterally. But when you see it in the context of this neighborhood, it makes so much sense to say that this is a gabled house and a singular volume. Yet you've concealed five dramatically different units within; there are little hints where you start to suggest ways in which you can perceive the fact that this isn't a single-family residence, but those are very subtle secondary readings.

Where the House on a Slope might be read as having a shed roof, even though it is a gabled roof, I almost misread the Concord House as having a hip roof because of the angle that occurs at the intersection and bend of the two volumes. This is the first of several interesting misreadings.

It is difficult to decipher where that boundary between the two volumes actually occurs, as you see certain architectural elements on one geometry and other elements on a different geometry. There isn't a common and unifying seam between the two, but more of a slip. This is further complicated by the fact that the house contains three residential units, not two or one.

Jeannette Kuo   In all three cases, though in very different ways, we're quite intensively dealing with this idea of the context and what image actually fits within that context. It is partially about this idea of the suburban and its ordinariness, and what is appropriate within that context, but it also explores how you break down something that maybe is bigger than it should be, or bigger than you want it to be perceived, so that, in fact, it could be experienced differently.

As you mentioned, Bryan, we're all of a similar generation, one that is past that notion of "fuck context." We're past that state of having everything be just purely formally expressive and bombastic, but rather we try to sneak in an agenda through these ambiguous moments. Something may look like it is completely ordinary, but then you take a second glance and you realize it's really quite strange.

Sean Canty   In all three projects there's the image of type as well as the organization of type. I think we're each working with both of those things in very similar ways, particularly in terms of context. Jeannette, I'm so curious about your House on a Slope, where in some cases the organization of the units seems very much determined by the site, the actual slope, while in other cases you're sneaking in some of these other models of inhabitation in the area.

It's perhaps more historically tied to a particular way of inhabiting space. There's an incredible amount of variety in the project in terms of the unit types, in terms of working with the slope, but also in the context, the image of the big gable, and the mapping of another typology of unit types into the interior of the project.

Jeannette Kuo   To a certain degree, we were trying to subvert what we typically expect of an apartment, to give spatial value to something that on paper would look like quite small apartments, but, because of the stepping, because of this form of the roof that gives it a different character, you start to find a generosity that you don't typically find in an apartment. That's the play with the typology.

Bryan Young   Part of what is interesting about context is that there are familiar reference points that establish related expectations for the built environment. Then the sneakiness happens. It is in the round geometrically for the Concord House and through the elevations and section in the case of the House on a Slope.

Sean Canty   Perhaps the mystery in the Concord House is in the concave and convex sides, the use of tangency, and the calibration of the angle of the cone and cylinder to the walls and the gables. You're not quite sure if it is a whole figure, because it's always partially disguised from either side. It's much more collective than something that's axial. It's something that has a center versus a gable that doesn't have a center. In the Six Square House, I find that the triangle at the center works in a similar way. As a figure, it accelerates and folds perspectives in a particular, almost Piranesian way. On the interior, spaces are constantly either turning towards you or away from you. Even though you're in one part of the house, you visually feel connected to the other side of the house.

Jeannette Kuo   It's the moment where you would expect it to be quite introverted. You expect the center to be a point of attention, but, in fact, it blasts the house open with a very strong centrifugal force of views toward the outside.

Sean Canty   The reflected ceiling plans of both the Concord House and the Six Square House are quite important, actually, as the plans don't do justice to what's happening spatially.

Bryan Young   At the Six Square House, the plan suggests separation of program while the ceiling creates smooth continuity. When you try to reconcile the plan and ceiling plan at the same time, it constructs a conundrum.

Sean, your comment about the relationship between a plan and reflected ceiling plan may be another methodological construct of our generation. I think we've learned to appreciate a clarity and rigor to a planning methodology. Yet, as the plan is realized, we're constantly in pursuit of something that may be less clear. At the Six Square House and the Concord House this is seen through incongruities of plan and ceiling plan, while at the House on a Slope this is more a complexity of program in the uniqueness of the layout of the five units.

Jeannette Kuo   Absolutely. I would even venture to say that if you looked at any single drawing that we've produced for each of these projects, it never tells the full story. You can't even use all the drawings to express what that space would feel like and the moments that you actually experience.

With the House on a Slope, many people misunderstand it as having quite constricted spaces. In plan it seems so compact, like we're jamming all these things in, but when they go to visit it, they're surprised how tall the ceilings are and that, through the stepping, they get a very different feel of how they engage with the space.

Both of your projects similarly shape very unexpected moments, even though, from the outside, there's a certain sense of calmness about them. There's an acceptance of a convention and local vernacular, you could say, but from these somehow it gets tweaked and becomes complex as you move from the exterior to the interior.

Bryan Young   Despite similarities across these three projects, I was struck by how the roofs are functioning in very different ways. In the Concord House, I feel the roof is a fifth facade, while in the House on a Slope, the roof is a cap or lid that pulls five different elements together. In the Six Square House, the roof is a shifting registration of geometric continuity.

Jeannette Kuo   In Sean's case, to make a uniform reading, the house needs to look like a solid mass, but you then start to see a Boolean object where the distinct volumes start to merge together in the joint.

Sean Canty   It tries to appropriate certain kinds of stereotomic techniques, something that is carved away, while also dealing with the realities of how we build things today.

Bryan, in the Six Square House, there seems to be a doubling of your roof from the outside versus the inside. And sometimes the two are closely mapped together; you can see the edge dipping on the exterior and then you find it on the interior. In other moments, however, there's a mismapping between the two, particularly in the living room, where the ceiling ridges make it feel so volumetric, which seems almost impossible because, from the exterior, it feels too thin.

Bryan Young   That's right. Most of the roof sections are going to have a very consistent and faithful thickness between the ceiling plane and the roof plane that is simply the various layers of assembly. But there are moments in which these two planes separate as the ceiling geometry negotiates the room configurations in a manner that is necessarily different than the exterior geometry on the roof. To say that more clearly, the roof is an immediate translation of geometries of the plan's squares with continuous eaves along the elevations; while the ceiling mostly follows this geometry, it also unexpectedly strays at moments to construct new and critical lines of tangency and continuity along the interior.

Sean Canty   The continuous and the discrete are always fighting it out, and this moment in the living room is the pressure point where those two things meet in such a wonderful way, a moment of shared tendency in-between the plan and section of the project.

Bryan Young   There's a friction in that resolution, as if we established certain geometric principles and then strayed from them and tried to resolve them again through geometry. I think that also happens at the rotunda of the Concord House.

Jeannette Kuo   This is also an issue of ambiguity, not just about the image, but also in the different ways that we read something that is very thin and surface-like and something very massive and volumetric.

Bryan Young   Themes that keep coming up in our conversation are references and being sneaky. Jeannette's House on a Slope is a multifamily dwelling with five units, yet provocatively disguises itself as a single building. And Sean's Concord House has three units but reads as singular. At times you can begin to sense a duality, but you very rarely reveal the fact that this has three units. On the other hand, Young Projects was given a program for a single-family house, but we began with a very conscious effort to aggregate the elements into a tight cluster. And so, it seems to me that there is a resistance in all of us; we've all taken our given programs and site conditions and confused the resolutions relative to part-to-whole relationships. Are these approaches generational?

> Jeannette Kuo   I definitely think that we're all fascinated by something that you can't understand in one go. I think we were trained, through the generation before us, to think about the singularity of a concept, defining from the top down what the constitutions of a project would be. Every element of a design would in essence respect this overall concept, and that difference gets subsumed within a singular idea.
> Perhaps the fascination of our generation is not having a singular idea. There's still a concept that ties it all together, but that concept is more loose, it allows for difference. . .

Bryan Young   . . . a multitude of readings that don't necessarily have to reinforce a singular idea. As you immerse yourself within a highly charged spatial environment, or due to highly charged material innovation, what you initially perceive is almost always not what it turns out to be.
That doesn't mean that the conclusion for our work has to bring these contradictory readings back to a singular understanding. In fact, I think it's important that it opens it up to understanding a variety of ways in which it can be interpreted.

> Jeannette Kuo   There's also a certain acceptance that things just don't need to be completely resolved.

Sean Canty   This not only invites a closer reading of these architectures, but also allows for them to be read by audiences without a high literacy in what we do; they will understand that something is not quite what it appears to be. I think that's also our responsibility as architects—to teach through what we do and how we do it.

I'm slightly younger than you both, and I suppose my work is in some ways also pushing back against the focus of my education, which was at the height of the digital and the parametric. Everything had to be articulated and clear in terms of process. Perhaps some of the ambiguity you see in my work is part of resisting a lot of that.

Jeannette Kuo   I feel like Bryan and I might be on the front end, and you're more at the tail end of that generation, when there was a euphoria about parametrics. And the following generation never lived without the 3-D. We're perhaps then the half-generation, which feels a renewed sense of constructive reality. To a certain degree the driving question is, "How do you actually make this thing?" The way in which we've engaged with geometry in these three houses has to do with a fascination about geometry, but also shows a distrust of geometry resolving itself constructively.

Ultimately, I think our generation doesn't have a fixed reference. We're omnivorous in the sense that we reference everything, but not any one thing. I think we're floating in between all of these different languages, and we've almost merged those types of things that we've learned and that still are part of our collective baggage.

There is always an alternative path that is more difficult to find, "less trodden," as the poem goes, but infinitely more pleasurable.

This is the path that Bryan Young has taken since his master's thesis project at Harvard University, and even if each of his projects have gone in a formally different direction, they have all converged at a point of pleasure that is rare in architecture. Importantly, and with every project, Young takes this approach with the full mastery of having navigated the main path and knowing to where it leads, like an animal who has known the security of domestication but who always returns to the rapture of wilderness.

When Donkey Kong is mapped into an architectural space, an architecture that has dictated spatiality and circulation, the beast obviously messes things up. He destroys Mario's buildings, but he also opens spatial possibilities and passages that one could not have seen in Mario's version of the world. Perhaps in some ways this approaches glitch art, an art form that turns mistakes and bugs into avenues for innovation within the systemically developed digital space. But there is more in Young Projects' approach than the glitch. Bryan does not see a distinction between the glitch and the bit. Every bit could be turned into a glitch if one only anticipates the other possibilities that could unfold, the other paths that could be taken at every instance.

Young's Donkey Kong/Pac-Man thesis project comments upon the diagrammatic approach to architecture that prevailed in the first decades of this century and continues to influence our formal strategies in design today. According to this approach, architecture needs to provide a diagrammatic abstraction to the program and circulation which then translates with graphic clarity into form. This approach to form uses three main strategies: separate and clearly sequestered spaces are directly related to separate functions; extrusion of the plan extends and maintains the two-dimensional diagrammatic clarity in the third dimension; and a sharply delineated path weaves through the plan and section to guide the user through the complexities of program (read: life). Yet, instead of an extrusion that only confirms the diagram, Young finds glitches, disturbances, and hinges among the 2-D space that rescue the princess and the player from the tediousness and predictability of the diagrammatic layout and the path the player takes through

it. The path leads nowhere if it does not lead to liberation from itself by virtue of making it more complex or hovering above or within its own depth, being on and off at the same time. It requires a cunning mind to be able to set the rules of the game and to also break them. This is the allegorical tension between Mario as the builder and Donkey Kong as the destroyer, or rather the explorer, of alternative 3-D paths across 2-D mazes.

In every project since, Young has demonstrated a similarly strong mastery of current norms of form and a deep engagement in the debates of contemporary architecture. He plays very well by the rules and plays even better around them, laterally, through wit and humor, reminding us of the pleasures that architecture evinces if it only held on to its exploratory spirit, rather than just its rules and complexities.

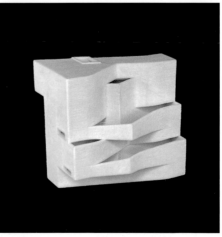

Bryan Young, "UpUpDownDownLeftRightLeft," 2003.

In that sense, the work exposes countless delights about architecture and how it opens up possibilities for life to be more indulgent and wild. Bryan's approach is not unlike those that the Fauves (literally "wild beasts" in French) artists and then the Nabis artists exposed in modern art, when they took painting to the lushness of the interior and to the garden. In that, they carved out an entirely different, parallel, and blissfully pleasurable path for modernism, which architecture has yet to find.

Starting with artists such as Henri Matisse and André Derain, Fauvism maintained a strong momentum throughout the 20th century and a steady influence on modern art, not as the mainstream but as the alternative path that embraced the hedonisms of form and mapped them onto the hedonisms of life. Among artists today, the work of David Hockney and Howard Hodgkin comes to mind as having continued that path. For some reason, architecture never had its explicitly Fauvist moment. However, if we look searchingly, we can find some suggestive indulgences, even if not directly linked to Fauvism, in some of the work of late modernists who introduced mannerism into the rules of their own game, like the late Le Corbusier, or some of the latter-day Italian rationalists like Ignazio Gardella, Luigi Moretti, or Luigi Caccia Dominioni. There may be an overlap between these strategies and the escapism of the high bourgeoisies, but we should also not forget that the craft of the Fauves lay in turning modest interiors and landscape into lush spaces and, accordingly, in amplifying the little gratifications of life into big pleasures.

Similar skills are deployed in the houses of Young Projects, starting with the careful selection and framing of the subject matter, the quiet voluptuous luxury in which the houses bathe. In every interior, he painstakingly calibrates enclosure and openness. We are always unsure as to whether we are looking at an enclosing plane or through it, whether it is a wall or a window, the window being at once the barrier and link between the lush interior and its feral counterpart. There is enough of each to create a sense of withdrawal, a temporary retreat away from the mundaneness and monotony of the quotidian, and a projection into a new setting which is only the old setting but differently framed. Along the way, Young at once

Hashim Sarkis

André Derain, 1906, *Charing Cross Bridge, London*,
Musée d'Orsay

David Hockney, 2017, *A Bigger Interior With Blue
Terrace and Garden*, Private collection

Retreat House, Dominican Republic

embraces and challenges the very aesthetics and effects of the conventional standards of interior comfort.

A related but slightly different strategy is that of unfolding, how he turns two dimensions into three dimensions not by extrusion alone but by angling and connecting these two-dimensional surfaces as if by hinges and opening them wide. The wide angles allow a space to be quasi-enclosed but also to point obliquely to outside the enclosure. Here we detect techniques similar to the recent work of Hockney, particularly his interiors/exteriors paintings, where the space unfolds into a visual journey not just a view. By a careful rotation of surfaces and calibrated overlaps between them, each view proposes alternative paths to the depths of a dining room or the uncharted seductions of the garden. However, a glitch is carefully constructed into the perspective, a secret door that could alternatively lead you to the depths of the dining room and the seductions of the garden. Through unexpected perspectives, spatial inversions and overlaps, and hidden portals Young constructs lush interiors/exteriors to be experienced as a narrative of shifting settings continuously reframed and occasionally revealing new worlds.

In Young's work, these surfaces elude flatness through another technique. They acquire rich textures so that the eye moves not only along them but into their depths and then from one intense texture to another. In projects like the Glitch House, these textured surfaces accrete into a wilderness that does not pretend to relate to the wilderness of the city or the forest beyond, but only insofar as the blue scales of the lizard's skin, as artificial as blue is, plays an important part in its camouflage effect; and only insofar as the intersection of two regular, flat patterns produces a wildly irregular and deep space. Every surface is not a surface, it is an exploration of a thin depth, juxtaposed against another.

Even more so, there is the notion of the cutout, as in the Six Square House, where the forms could be seen as unfolding spaces, but the calibration of their rotation produces other, more powerful figures in between. A triangle with curved edges emerges not to spoil the square but to confirm and exaggerate the sense of its rotation. It moves even if it is still. This technique is

Wild Beast

Six Square House, Bridgehampton, New York

also applied in the design of objects, like the bench in the Rock House bath and the Elephant Table, which appear to be scenes from a life from multiple points of view, as if a conversation is playing itself out in still life.

Another wild beast that inhabits the work of Young Projects is that of the ghost in the machine. If the ghost of Derain was the colorful smoke that unexpectedly spewed from the dreary factory, Young's ghosts for the fourth machine age are human hands that dabble in the same level of autonomy and parametrics as the computer, producing unexpected, randomized patterns. Against the obsession of leaving the willful hand out so that even the random and the authored is simulated through a rationality, Young puts his hand in the process of making to twist the form and generate anomalies within the corresponding matter. In the patterns of the Pulled Plaster House, a randomness that was supposed to be produced by a set of parameters which simulate the randomness of the human hand is here produced by the human hand inserted in the machine. This is not the hand of Ruskin's stone masons. It is the hand of the machine operator or of the writer of the code and it is not there to express human labor as much as to celebrate human wit. No matter how perfect the machine is in simulating randomness and replacing the hand, the mind that drives the hand will always be able to outsmart it.

Afterall, Young is the master of the willful glitch. Breaking the rules is too easy for him, too rough. He does not break the rules but writes into them the possibilities and pleasures of them breaking themselves or breaking down. His architecture is at once a representation of life as it is as, with its rules, rhythms, interiors, exteriors, privacies, and decorums, and of life as it could be if we only allow for glitches, or windows into other possibilities that it could have been. Such is the pleasure of aesthetic experience, and no one has been exploring the techniques of pleasure in contemporary architecture as rigorously and as joyfully as Bryan Young.

Young Projects has been extremely fortunate to have clients willing to take risks—often in their own homes. We owe an enormous thank you to all our clients who have made these projects possible, especially Mia Jung and Scott Lawin, and Chris Canavan and Colleen Foster. The oldest and newest, the largest and smallest projects featured in *Figure—Cast—Frame* are the result of an ongoing collaboration with Sukey Novogratz and Mike Novogratz; it is impossible to thank you enough for giving us our break and continuing to encourage new ideas.

Starting an office in New York City in 2010 necessitated finding small opportunities within each job, projects within projects. As presented throughout this book, these moments have frequently been the result of working directly with builders and artisans to create something unexpected. Cheers to the millworkers, metal workers, plaster masters, concrete casters, furniture fabricators, and many others who opened their doors and blew our minds.

We have been lucky to run with tireless and fearless designers, both within Young Projects and through various consultations across disciplines. Thank you to all our past and current employees, interns, freelancers, and consultants (especially Nat Oppenheimer). A special thanks to Noor Alawadhi, who pushed this book forward from the very start and to partner Mallory Shure, whose impact on the office has allowed us to grow immensely. An extra special thanks to partner Noah Marciniak, who coauthored *Figure—Cast—Frame* and has been fundamental to the conception and resolution of all our young projects. (Also, thanks to Noah's family—Karyn, Hazel, and baby Etta, who have patiently put up with some long hours and potentially obsessive behavior.)

The book's contributors—Nader Tehrani, Dana Barnes, Paola Lenti, Jeannette Kuo, Sean Canty, and Hashim Sarkis—inspired us to further examine our process and revealed unforeseen connections across our broader body of work. The themes presented here are in many ways the result of your insights. We are immensely indebted to you for your thoughtfulness. Thank you to editor Julia van den Hout who cut through some vague ambiguities and brought to light more relevant and crisp oscillations (and maybe ambiguities). Julia also guided our effort at every step of the way and quite simply made the monograph happen. We are deeply appreciative to book designer Luke Bulman who translated the intertwined ideas into a visual narrative, highlighting the work with graphic clarity and elegance. Lastly, thank you to Alan Rapp, The Monacelli Press, and Phaidon for believing in this monograph.

Thank you to the many employers for rigorous training over a solid decade, especially the late Roddy Creedon of Allied Architecture and Design; Jane Cee and Peter Pfau of Cee/Pfau Collaborative; Stephen Cassell, Adam Yarinsky, and Kim Yao of Architecture Research Office (ARO); and Brad Cloepfil and Kyle Lommen of Allied Works Architecture.

My brother Michael Young has helped explain these projects within the discourse of contemporary architecture and the context of scientist rock. I'm grateful to my parents Jacky and Greg and my brother John for the constant support. *Figure—Cast—Frame* was largely written and assembled while working remotely during the pandemic. Thank you to my daughter Marlo for getting me out of my head and my wife Marina for putting up with it for so long. I love you dearly.

Hive Lamp

The Hive Lamp pretends to be related to a beehive as it is suspended from a thin stem among a small grouping of birch trees on a roof top in Lower Manhattan. The lamp consists of three spiraling lobes whose symmetry is obscured by a cellular network of hexagons that morph across its surface. The packed cells form a structural skin and veil a soft light that emanates from the three seeds at the center.

Status: built prototype
Location: New York, New York
Year: 2010
Collaborator: Michael Young
Fabricator: Polich Tallix
Photos: Young Projects

Retreat House

Located on an undeveloped site in the Dominican Republic, the Retreat House is designed to take full advantage of the pristine beachscape at the front of the property, balancing expansive views of the Atlantic Ocean with the experience of the lush, dense jungle that dominates the majority of the site.

Status: built
Location: Dominican Republic
Year: 2019
Size: 20,000 sf
Type: hospitality
Builders: Gentry Construction, IMODOM, Vanderhorst Vanderhorst y Asociados
Structure: Robert Silman Associates
Interiors: Young Projects and Sukey Novogratz with Colony Design

Local Architect: Estudio Sarah Garcia
Landscaping: Green Paisajismo
Special thanks: Oak Gentry, Chris Layton, Mauricio Rojas, Sarah Garcia, Desiree Casoni, Jon Cielo, Meredith Kole, Mark Watanabe, Nat Oppenheimer and Jeff Beane, Natalia Franch, Ysabela Molini, Jean Lin, Roberto Ruiz Vargas, Isaac Vanderhorst, Renan Vanderhorst, Ali, and Fausto
Photos: Iwan Baan and Karla Read

Wythe Corner House

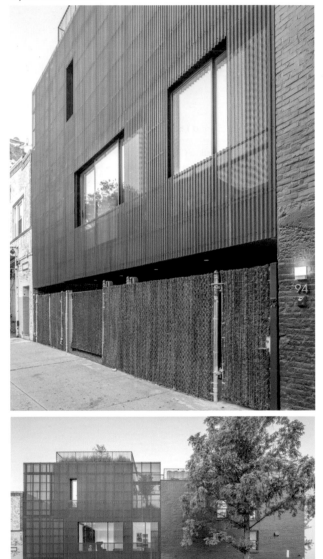

The Wythe Corner House involved a gut renovation and modern addition to an early 1900s townhouse on a corner lot in Williamsburg. The addition's massing proposes a radical break from Brooklyn's traditional townhouse addition typology. Rather than equally divide the available floor area at each level or simply prioritize a larger lower addition, the design distributes all available area on the second and third floors.

Status: built
Location: Brooklyn, New York
Year: 2014
Size: 2,000 sf existing and 1,500 sf addition
Type: mixed use
Builder: Advanced Building Contractors
Structure: Robert Silman Associates
MEP: Engineering Solutions
Landscape Architecture: Bau Land
Special thanks: Mark Watanabe, John Ryan, Gerry, Jan, and Emily
Photos: Alan Tansey

Pulled Plaster House

The Pulled Plaster House occupies 6,000 interior square feet and 1,500 square feet of roof garden on the top two floors and roof of a historic building. The proposal explores shifting relationships of solid and void through the interplay of three distinct nested prisms. The renovation features the modified technique of pulling plaster to create a series of undulating and textured plaster tiles.

Status: built
Location: New York, New York
Year: 2015
Size: 5,000 sf
Type: residential
Builder: Taocon
Structure: Robert Silman Associates
MEP: Engineering Solutions
Landscape architecture: Future Green Studio
Plaster research and prototype: Hyde Park Mouldings
Screen fabrication: Kammetal
Special thanks: Jon Cielo, Jon, Steven, Tim
Photos: Naho Kubota, Young Projects, and Desiree Casoni

Hamptons House

The Hamptons Bungalow is a year-round retreat located on a 1-acre site in Westhampton. The compact and linear front facade maintains a low horizontal profile with a roof line that rises 8 feet above a monolithic concrete foundation. Upon entering the house, a series of folded ceiling planes slope upward to full-height operable glass windows facing the south (pool) and west (deck).

Status: built
Location: Westhampton, New York
Year: 2014
Type: 2,100 sf
Type: ground-up residential
Builder: Vital Habitats
Structure: Robert Silman Associates
Special thanks: Marina Vidal-Young, Marlo Young, Kim, Charles, and Judy
Photos: Costas Picadas

Elephant Table

The Elephant Table is a family of six similar stones. Related in form and aesthetic origin, the six pieces are individual elements which together to compose an imperfect yet complete whole, or clustered in a variety of manners. The table is fabricated from milled quartzite and limestone.

Status: built
Year: 2017
Fabricator and collaborator: Quarra Stone
Special thanks: Sina Özbudun, Brad Isnard, Brian Smith, Brian Kehoe, James Durham
Photos: Chris Hynes Photography

Rock House

The Rock House program includes an open-air massage space accessed from the beach, a steam room, cold plunge pool, hammam, dry sauna, and climate-controlled changing room. The form of the spa allows for the reading of a singular space despite the varying parameters of each adjacent program.

Status: unbuilt
Location: Dominican Republic
Year: 2016
Size: 1,900 sf
Type: hospitality
Structure: Robert Silman Associates
MEP: Arup
Spa: 4Seasons Spa
Special thanks: Sina Özbudun, Sonya Ursell, Noor Alawadhi

Match Maker Heart

The Match-Maker Heart cosmically connected strangers throughout the month of February in Times Square, New York. Guided by their zodiac sign, visitors arrange themselves at twelve points around the heart-shaped sculpture. Peering through colorful, interwoven periscopes provides glimpses of each viewer's four most ideal astrological mates, offering potential novel connections between lonely souls or settled lovers.

Status: built
Location: New York, New York
Year: 2014
Type: folly
Graphic Design: Once Future
Structure: Robert Silman Associates
Lighting: Doug Russell/Lighting Workshop
Fabricator: Kammetal
Client: Times Square Arts and Van Alen Institute
Special thanks: Noah Marciniak, Alastair Kusack, Sam Kusack, David van der Leer, Sherry Dobbin
Photos: Sean Hemmerle

Glitch House

The Glitch House is the first structure a guest sees upon arriving at the Wellness Retreat. Rather than marking this moment with a defined boundary, the Glitch House strangely smears itself into the jungle landscape. It is a hint towards the immersive experiences that guides the design for the Retreat in general.

Status: built
Location: Dominican Republic
Year: 2018
Size: 3500 sf
Type: ground-up residential
Builder: Gentry Construction, Vanderhorst Vanderhorst y Asociados
Special thanks: Bastian Feltgen, Aguayo Tiles
Photos: Iwan Baan and Karla Read

The Kitchen

The Kitchen, pioneer of New York's avant-garde scene from 1971 onward, conducted an invited competition to reconsider and expand the offices, galleries, and performance spaces it has called home since 1987. To facilitate the evolving requirements of the nonprofit's various programs, we proposed a small performance theater as a rooftop addition, and redesigned the building's lobby, circulation core, and common spaces.

Status: invited competition
Location: New York, New York
Year: 2015
Size: 30,000 sf
Type: renovation and addition of art institution
Special thanks: Sina Özbudun, Sonya Ursell, Nathan Frey

Carraig Ridge Fireplace

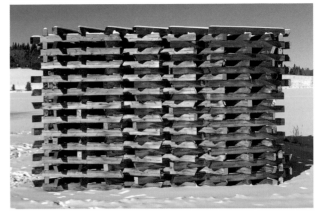

With a limited design schedule of just four weeks, it was important to develop a straightforward method of construction using readily available materials. As such, the Carraig Ridge Fireplace is constructed of stacked, heavy, Douglas Fir timber cut into lengths of 3-to-5-feet and arranged into any of six unique positions based on a rotation, creating a subtle twist around the center. This playful interpretation of stacked firewood produces a thick yet porous veil between the cubic exterior and cylindrical interior.

Status: built
Location: Alberta, Canada
Year: 2014
Size: 400 sf
Type: folly
Builder: Carraig Ridge
Special thanks: Ian MacGregor and Kate MacGregor
Photos: Brett Bilon and Bent Rene Synnevag, courtesy of Carraig Ridge, Young Projects

The Snow Queen

In 2015, Young Projects was invited to design an installment of Kate Bernheimer's Fairy Tale Architecture, an ongoing series that explores the relationship between the realms of fairy tales and architecture. As illustrations for the Hans Christian Andersen story "The Snow Queen," we documented the swarm formations of magnetic filaments frozen in resin casts. (Resin Bees)

Type: illustrations for *Places Journal*
Special thanks: Andy Bernheimer, Kate Bernheimer, Cassandra Beaudry, Sarah Mogensen

Project Credits

Retreat Guest House

The Guest House is sited at the periphery of a natural jungle clearing as part of the Retreat in the Dominican Republic. The building is a series of four identical mirrored suites unified under a single arcing roof. The suites' rotating orientations alternate the views of each suite to align with one of two magnificent Ficus trees. While the trees provide reference points to align the suites, the center of the clearing serves as the center of the arc of the roof.

Status: built
Location: Dominican Republic
Year: 2019
Size: 2,500 sf
Type: ground-up hospitality
Builder: Gentry Construction, IMODOM, Vanderhorst Vanderhorst y Asociados
Landscaping: Green Paisajismo
Special thanks: Jon Cielo, Bastian Feltgen, Sina Özbudun
Photos: Iwan Baan

Houses in the Block

Houses on the Block revisits a mini-tower as a charged architectural parti. The plan consists of a super small core with elevator, egress, and utilities, leaving the rest of the plan free for residential and common programming. Each apartment is designed to maximize daylight, ventilation, and livability. The units are varied and unique to accommodate extended family living, seniors or live-work lifestyles that are often overlooked by market-driven developments.

Status: unbuilt
Location: New York, New York
Year: 2018
Special thanks: Brad Isnard, Elias Bey, Noor Alawadhi

Mali Museum

The organizing principles of our proposal for the New Contemporary Art Wing are based upon the plan inversions of two mirrored ellipses creating a structural and conceptual grid. The geometric logic of the ellipse, its curve orbiting two focal points, allows the New Contemporary Art Wing to stand in contrast to the orthogonal, rectilinear logic of the existing historic Palacio de la Exposición. This critical difference allows the proposed New Wing to achieve a perceivable iconic identity despite being significantly less visible than the Palacio.

Status: unbuilt
Location: Lima, Peru
Year: 2015
Size: 80,000 sf
Type: art museum
Special thanks: Bastian Feltgen, Sina Özbudun

Cage Shelving

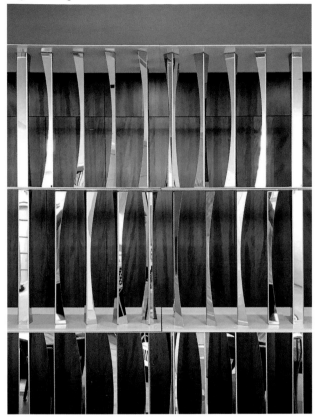

One module measures 16 inches-by-18-inches-by-48 inches (combination of six modules shown). The modules can be combined (flipped) in any orientation. The shelving is self-supporting as a freestanding object and a screen, made of polished stainless steel and powder coated steel. Custom colors and finishes are available.

Status: built
Location: Brooklyn, New York
Year: 2019
Fabrication: Kammetal
Special thanks: Ines Hernandez, Jason, and Leslie

Six Square House

Located on a 2-acre lot adjacent to a historic house in Bridgehampton, the Six Square House is made up of six 24-foot-square modules

each featuring a gabled geometry. The six modules are composed to create structural continuity between exterior roof ridges, while roof eaves flow upward and downward along curves to break from the traditional typology of a gabled barn.

Status: built
Location: Bridgehampton, New York
Year: 2020
Size: 3,500 sf
Type: single family ground-up residential
Builder: Taconic
Structure: Robert Silman Associates
Landscape Architecture: Coen+Partners
Landscaping: Landscape Details
Rainscreen: reSAWN
Millwork: Chapter & Verse, Swiss Woodcraft
Styling: Matter Made
Special thanks: Rachel Lee, Sonya Ursell, Shane Coen, Roy, John M, John P, Jamie, Amauri, Lisa and Billy, Connor, and Joseph
Photos: Alan Tansey, Matter Made, Lifestyle Production Group

The Wells

Young Projects' Young Projects

As a structure, Wells Center can be read as a sculptural mass of petrified wood or a fairy tale found object. Programmatically there are three distinct cylinder-like wellness chambers: a sound bath, a salt bath, and a sweat bath (kiva). In addition to these three "wells," an existing subterranean concrete vault is reprogrammed as a meditation and yoga room with a changing area, shower, and water closet. The south/east side of the vault has been excavated and glazed to allow the entry of morning light and a new sunken patio.

Status: unbuilt
Location: Amagansett, New York
Year: 2019
Special thanks: Noor Alawadhi, Elias Bey, Matthew Jones

Young Projects' Young Projects are a series of form finding material experiments that may be conducted at home under adult supervision. The first YPYP grew saline and epsom salt crystals along complex lattice networks made of thin thread. Through the crystal growth, lines of tension transform to compression and become increasingly thick and rigid at nodes and corners; providing a organically formed efficient structural diagram.

Type: salt structures
Special thanks: Elias Bey, Ozzy

Lacehouse

A wedged, post-industrial site along the Bow River in Calgary lies at the periphery of the modern business district, but at the hub of a network of parks, trails, and pedestrian bridges that link to quiet residential neighborhoods. The form of Lace House is guided by zoning rules that encourage the development of an urban street-wall on the city side but mandate wedding-cake setbacks along the riverfront. Prefabricated facade panels of equal dimension wrap the unequal lengths of facade that are tailored to the zoning envelope. The discontinuous grid of the facade could be read as an adaptation of the modernist project, distorted or corrupted to fit its hybrid context.

Status: unbuilt
Location: Calgary, Canada
Year: 2019
Size: 70,000 sf
Type: mixed use
Special thanks: Noor Alawadhi

Tile Prototypes

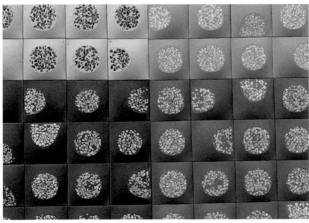

In 2020, Young Projects began collaborating with the Italian design and furniture company Paola Lenti, founded in 1994 in Meda. The ongoing partnership produced two prototypes in 2021, entitled "cluster" and "tilt."

Status: built prototypes available for purchase
Year: 2021
Special thanks: Roberto Orsi, Kicco Bestetti, Noor Alawadhi, Paola Lenti, Anna Lenti
Photos: Paola Lenti

Steelcase Work Life Center

After a pause due to the pandemic, construction began on the renovation of Steelcase's Work Life center located in Columbus Circle, New York. The renovation includes design of the 40,000-square-foot retail showroom of work environments occupying the sixth, seventh, and eighth floors adjacent to Central Park. The design for the showroom considers the myriad of shifting conditions Steelcase is addressing as the pandemic continues to shift the nature of work environments.

Status: under construction
Location: New York, New York
Year: 2022
Size: 35,000 sf
Type: showroom and office
Builder: JRM Construction Management
Structure: Robert Silman Associates
Lighting: One Lux Studio
Special thanks: Mallory Shure, Addy, Cherie, James, Brian
Photos: Young Projects

Tribeca Pied-à-Terre

A small but potent jewel-box studio renovation of 500 square feet. The project is defined by an immersive, highly sculptural plaster ceiling, whose soft peaks and honed ridges mark the realization of extensive material experiments by Young Projects. An elaborately veined burl wood volume containing a bed and closet complements the plaster canopy's graphic topography, while deep teal walls, cerulean tiling, and a sleek brushed-aluminum kitchenette add acute dimensionality.

Status: built
Location: New York, New York
Year: 2021
Size: 500 sf
Type: residential gut renovation

Builder: Think Construction
Plaster: Nathan Frey Plaster
Millwork: Chapter & Verse
Special thanks: Johan Kinnucan, Billy Hutton, Noor Alawadhi, Tim White
Photos: Alan Tansey

Cut Out House

The Cut Out House is a single family home located in a nature-oriented, low-density development in the foothills of the Canadian Rocky Mountains near Banff National Park. The two-story house steps to hug the steep topography of the site and minimize the bulk of the building while fully optimizing the opportunities for spectacular panoramic views. The primary architectural gesture of the building is a butterfly roof with a single valley running diagonally from corner to corner of the plan, terminating in an articulated fascia following the house's facades and curving to create a circular entry court.

Status: on the boards
Location: Alberta, Canada
Year: 2022
Size: 2,500 sf
Type: ground-up residential
Builder: Brookwright Developments
Special thanks: Kate MacGregor, Doug, Karen, Kirsten

Box Out Apartment

Perched atop a 9-story prewar red brick building, this zinc-clad penthouse apartment, made up of three smaller units merged into a two floor-duplex with a wrap-around terrace and direct views of Lincoln Center. Young Project's gut renovation connects the lower bedroom level with two feature stair volumes up to a new upper terrace. Floor to ceiling windows, shades of grey millwork, exposed concrete beams and blackened steel, transform a traditional shell into a modern loft-like refuge.

Status: under construction
Location: New York, New York
Year: 2022
Size: 4,000 sf
Type: residential gut renovation
Builder: Black Square
Structure: Blue Sky Design
MEP: ANZ Consulting Engineers
Landscape: Elevations Landscape Design + Build
Lighting: The SEED
Special thanks: Aileen, Chris, Mallory Shure, Billy Hutton, Jim, and Wojciech

The Fields

The Fields master plan is a 19-acre site in the Rocky Mountains that offers a departure from typical single-unit suburban sprawl. Balancing density with maximized open space, 135 residential units are clustered together to balance varying degrees of privacy and intimacy. Four typologies of units abut a generous and diverse parkscape running along the spine of the site. Principal design considerations include aggressively sustainable design and pre-fabricated timber construction techniques.

Status: on the boards
Location: El Jebel, Colorado
Year: 2023
Size: 19 acres and 135 units
Type: residential
Special thanks: Matthew Jones, Johan Kinnucan, Evan, and Jon

Four Square House

The Four Square House is a gut renovation of a historic 1820s Spanish Creole cottage and guesthouse in the French Quarter of New Orleans. The property includes a walled courtyard, large pool, three-bedroom main house, and two-bedroom guest house with a gallery that overlooks the courtyard. A four-square grid houses the primary programs—bar, music room, salon, and dinning room. The four adjacent rooms are treated as distinct volumes varying in hues, finish, material, and furnishings.

Status: under construction
Location: New Orleans, Louisiana
Year: 2021
Size: 5,000 sf
Type: residential renovation
Builder: Chris Layton and Kent Wells
Plaster and gold leaf: Madilynn Nelson
Landscape: Bureau Bas Smets
Special thanks: Billy Hutton, Caroline Ferguson, Chris, Kent, Tommy, and Victor

Carbondale Box

When complete, our design for this 30,000-square-foot mixed use building will be the first of its kind in the historic town of Carbondale, Colorado. Arranged above a commercial ground level, the building's four townhomes are generous in plan, with parking, storage, and exterior private amenity spaces. Both residential and commercial areas acknowledge the town's mining history and historic masonry buildings through the application of tactile, solid structural systems, and materials such as masonry and exposed mass timber elements.

Status: on the boards
Location: Carbondale, Colorado
Year: 2022
Size: 25,000 sf
Type: mixed use
Special thanks: Johan Kinnucan, Rosannah Harding, Evan, and Gavin

Saint Kitts Wellness Retreat

Design development has begun on our new hospitality project: the 40,000-square-foot resort and clubhouse, which includes a boutique hotel, 100-person event space and terrace, ocean-view swimming pool, spa, yoga terrace, and thirty-two freestanding one- and three-bedroom bungalows. Situated on a hillside with sweeping panoramic views of the Caribbean Sea, the stepped architecture plays an important role in allowing people to inhabit and traverse the steep site. Cascading horizontal datums in the form of floors and roofs emerge out of the terrain, creating perches to take in the stunning landscape.

Status: on the boards
Location: Saint Kitts and Nevis
Year: 2023
Size: thirty-two bungalows and 40,000 sf clubhouse
Type: hospitality
Structure: Robert Silman Associates
Special thanks: Rosannah Harding, Noor Alawadhi, Lan, and Bill

Image Credits

All photographs, drawings, diagrams, and other illustrative material not otherwise indicated below are © Young Projects. All other image credits that do not appear within the text are listed below, including material supplied by other institutions, agencies, or individuals.

All reasonable effort has been made to secure rights and permissions for all visual material. Any errors and omissions will be corrected in subsequent editions, provided notification is given to the publisher.

cover	© Juan Lopez-Spratt
3	© Iwan Baan
11	Top: Ground floor plan, Fisher House, Louis I. Kahn, 1967; redrawn by Young Projects
	Bottom: Final scheme, first floor plan, Dominican Motherhouse, Louis I. Kahn, 1968; redrawn by Michael Merrill and Ethan Yi Chiang
13	© Herzog & de Meuron
17	Top: © Iwan Baan
	Bottom: © Naho Kubota
18	Center: © Lifestyle Production Group
	Bottom: © Iwan Baan
20–1	© Iwan Baan
22–3	© Iwan Baan
24	© Iwan Baan
25	© Iwan Baan
27	© Iwan Baan
29	Bottom: © Iwan Baan
30–1	© Iwan Baan
32	© Iwan Baan
36–7	© Iwan Baan
39	© Iwan Baan
40–1	© Iwan Baan
43	Top and bottom: © Iwan Baan
48–9	© Iwan Baan
50	© Iwan Baan
51	© Iwan Baan
52	© Iwan Baan
53	© Iwan Baan
54	© Iwan Baan
55	© Iwan Baan
56–7	© Iwan Baan
62–3	© Iwan Baan
66–7	© Iwan Baan
68	© Iwan Baan
69	Top and bottom: © Iwan Baan
71	© Iwan Baan
72–3	© Iwan Baan
77	© Karla Read
79	© Iwan Baan
80–1	© Iwan Baan
83	© Iwan Baan
84	© Iwan Baan
85	© Iwan Baan
95	© Juan Lopez-Spratt
96–7	© Iwan Baan
99	© Bent Rene Synnevag, courtesy Carraig Ridge
101	© Bent Rene Synnevag, courtesy Carraig Ridge
102–3	© Bent Rene Synnevag, courtesy Carraig Ridge
104–5	© Bent Rene Synnevag, courtesy Carraig Ridge
106–7	© XYC Design & Development, courtesy Carraig Ridge
110	Top: © Iwan Baan
	Bottom: © Daniel Root
112	Left and right: © Daniel Root
115	© Daniel Root
116	© Daniel Root
120–1	© Naho Kubota
122	Left: Public Domain. Originally published in "The Work of George Edward Harding & Gooch," Architectural Record, July-September 1897, Volume 7, p.111; highlight by Young Projects
123	© Naho Kubota
124	© Naho Kubota
125	© Naho Kubota
126	© Naho Kubota
128–9	© Naho Kubota
132	© Naho Kubota
133	© Naho Kubota
144–5	© Naho Kubota
147	© Naho Kubota
159	© Alan Tansey
161	Bottom left and right: © Nathan Frey at MW plaster
163	© Alan Tansey
164	© Alan Tansey
165	© Alan Tansey
166–7	© Alan Tansey
185	© Chris Hynes Photography
186	© Karla Read
187	Top and bottom: © Chris Hynes Photography
188–9	© Chris Hynes Photography
191	Top left: © Maurizio Natta, top right: © Paola Lenti, photo

Library of Congress Control Number: 2021951968

ISBN 978-1-58093-598-2

10 9 8 7 6 5 4 3 2 1

Printed in China

Edited by Julia van den Hout, Original Copy

Design by Office of Luke Bulman

Monacelli
A Phaidon Company
65 Bleecker Street
New York, New York 10012

www.monacellipress.com